THE MIND OF ST PAUL

Professor Barclay was a distinguished scholar, an exceptionally gifted preacher and a regular broadcaster. His writings for the *British Weekly* were very popular and for twenty years from 1950 a full page every week was given to them. From 1963 until 1974 he was Professor of Divinity and Biblical Criticism at Glasgow University. He was a member of the Advisory Committee working on the New English Bible and also a Member of the Apocrypha Panel of Translators. In 1975 he was appointed a Visiting Professor at the University of Strathclyde for a period of three years where he lectured on Ethics, and in the same year—jointly with the Rev. Professor James Stewart—he received the 1975 Citation from the American theological organization The Upper Room; the first time it has been awarded outside America. His extremely popular *Bible Study Notes* using his own translation of the New Testament have achieved a world-wide sale.

Professor Barclay died in January 1978.

WILLIAM BARCLAY

The Mind of St Paul

Collins
FOUNT PAPERBACKS

First published by Wm. Collins Sons & Co Ltd 1958
First issued in Fontana Books 1965
Seventh Impression August 1974
Reprinted in Fount Paperbacks, January 1977
Tenth Impression January 1981

© William Barclay, 1958

Made and printed in Great Britain by
William Collins Sons & Co Ltd, Glasgow

CONTENTS

I   The Man of Two Worlds—The World of the Jew   9

II The Man of Two Worlds—The World of the Greek   17

III Paul's Thinking about God   26

IV The Divine Initiative   33

V   The Call of God   37

VI Paul's Thinking about Jesus Christ   42

VII The Incarnation   47

VIII The Work of Christ   55

IX The Death of Christ   74

X   The Risen Christ   83

XI In Christ   92

XII Paul's Conception of Faith   101

XIII The Essential Grace   117

XIV Paul's Thinking about the Holy Spirit   130

XV Paul's Thinking about Sin   138

XVI Paul's Conception of the Flesh   147

XVII The Second Coming in the Thought of Paul   156

XVIII The Mind of Paul Concerning the Church   174

PREFACE

These chapters originally appeared as a series of weekly articles in the pages of *The British Weekly*. I have to thank the previous editor of that paper, Rev. Shaun Herron, for giving me the opportunity to write them in the first place, and the present editor, Rev. Denis Duncan, for now giving me permission to republish them in book form. To the original series I have added two chapters, one on Sin and the other on the Church in the thinking of Paul.

These chapters do not in any way claim to be an exhaustive and complete Theology of Paul. I have simply gone direct to the Pauline letters to find out what Paul said and thought on certain great subjects. Their aim will be fulfilled, if they send people back to reading of Paul's letters themselves.

WILLIAM BARCLAY

Trinity College,
Glasgow,
February, 1958

I

THE MAN OF TWO WORLDS—
THE WORLD OF THE JEW

Christianity began with one tremendous problem. Clearly the message of Christianity was meant for all men. It was because God so loved the world that he sent his Son (*John* 3.16). It was Jesus' confidence that, if he was lifted up, he would draw all men unto him (*John* 12.32). The Church regarded it as her commission that she must go and teach all nations (*Matthew* 28.19). It was clear that Christianity had a message for all the world, and that unless that message was delivered, the Church would fail in her God-given duty.

But the fact remained that Christianity was cradled in Judaism; and, humanly speaking, no message which was meant for all the world could ever have had a more unfortunate cradle. The Jews were involved in a double hatred—the world hated them and they hated the world.

No nation was ever more bitterly hated than the Jews. Cicero called the Jewish religion "a barbarous superstition" (Cicero, *Pro Flacco* 28); Tacitus called the Jewish nation "the vilest of people" (Tacitus, *Histories* 5.8). Antisemitism is no new thing; it flourished in the ancient world.

No nation ever hated other nations as the Jews did. It is true that some few Jews held that the Jews were meant to be a light to the Gentiles to lead them to God; but for the most part the Jews were convinced that the fact that they were the chosen nation involved what to them was the equal and the opposite fact that all other nations were rejected nations. At their worst they could say : " The Gentiles were created by God to be fuel for the fires of hell." " The best of the serpents crush; the best of the Gentiles kill." It was even forbidden to give a Gentile mother help in her

9

hour of direst need, because to do so would only have been
to bring another Gentile into the world.

The Gentiles were acutely conscious of this hatred.
Tacitus believed that if a Gentile became a proselyte to
Judaism, the first thing he was taught was to despise the
gods, to repudiate his nationality, and to hold worthless his
parents, children and friends (Tacitus, *Histories* 5.5). Juvenal declared that if a Jew was asked the way to anywhere
by anyone, he would refuse all information except to a
fellow-Jew, and if anyone was looking for a well, he would
refuse to direct him to it, unless he was circumcised (Juvenal,
Satires, 14.103, 104).

In Alexandria the story was current that the Jews had
taken a deliberate oath never to show kindness to any
Gentile, and it was even said that the Jewish religious
ceremonies began with the yearly sacrifice of a Gentile
(Josephus, *Against Apion*, 2, 8, 10). The friends of Antiochus Sidetes urged him to exterminate the Jews because
" alone of all nations they refuse all fellowship and inter-
course with other nations and suppose all men to be
enemies " (Diodorus Siculus 31.1, 1). Josephus quotes the
charge of a certain Lysimachus that Moses charged the Jews
to show goodwill to no man, never to give good but always
evil counsel to others, and to overturn and destroy whatever
altars and temples of the gods they might encounter. Apion
himself affirmed that the Jews swore by the God of heaven
and earth and sea never to show good will to a man of
another nation, and especially never to do so to the Greeks
(Josephus, *Against Apion*, 1.34; 2.10).

The problem which faced Christianity was acute. It had
a message for all men; and yet in the eyes of the world it
was a Jewish thing, and the Jews were the most bitterly
hated and hating people in the ancient world.

Clearly one thing was necessary—a man who could somehow form a bridge between the Jewish and the Greek
worlds. Obviously such a man would be hard to find; such
a man would be unique; and yet, in the providence of God,
the hour produced the man—and that man was Paul.

In his life of Scott, Lockhart quotes a saying of an old

countryman about the way in which the lines of life had
fallen for Scott, and, in his *Life and Letters of Paul,* David
Smith took the saying as the very text for the life of Paul :
"He was makin' himsell a' the time; but he didna ken
maybe what he was about till years had passed." Life had
been moulding Paul to be the bridge between the Jews and
the Greeks, to be the unique channel through whom
Christianity went out to all the world.

First of all, let us look at Paul the Jew. To the end of his
life Paul was proudly, stubbornly, unalterably a Jew. When
he wrote to the Corinthians in answer to the charges of his
detractors, he took his stand on his Jewish lineage : "Are
they Hebrews? So am I. Are they Israelites? So am I.
Are they the seed of Abraham? So am I " (*II Corinthians*
11.22). The three words he uses all have their own meaning. A *Hebrew* was a Jew who could still speak Hebrew in
contradistinction to the Jews of the Dispersion who had
forgotten their native language for the Greek of their
adopted countries. An *Israelite* was specifically a member
of the covenant nation. To be *of the seed of Abraham* was
to have absolute racial purity. Paul's claim was that there
was nowhere in the world a purer Jew than he.

He made the same claim when he wrote to his friends
at Philippi : "If any other man thinketh that he hath
whereof he might trust in the flesh, I more; circumcised
the eighth day; of the stock of Israel; of the tribe of Benjamin, an Hebrew of the Hebrews; as touching the law, a
Pharisee; concerning zeal, persecuting the Church; touching
the righteousness which is in the law, blameless " (*Philippians* 3.4-6). When he wrote to the Church at Rome, he
made the proud statement : "I also am an Israelite, of the
seed of Abraham, of the tribe of Benjamin " (*Romans* 11.1).

Again and again Paul's Jewishness comes out. When he
was writing to Gentiles, the ancient Israelites are our fathers
(*I Corinthians* 10.1). Even writing to the Church at Rome,
Abraham is our father (*Romans* 4.1), as is also Isaac
(*Romans* 9.10). To Paul, the Church is the Israel of God
(*Galatians* 6.16). No passage in all Paul's letters throbs with
a greater intensity of feeling than the passage in *Romans*

where Paul cries out that he himself would gladly consent
to be accursed if he might only bring to belief his kinsmen
after the flesh (*Romans* 9.3). Paul's speeches in *Acts* paint
the same picture as his letters do. It is Paul's claim to the
military commander in Jerusalem : " I am a man which am
a Jew of Tarsus, a city in Cilicia " (*Acts* 21.39). The next
day, when he is under examination, it is his opening statement : " I am verily a man which am a Jew, born in Tarsus,
a city in Cilicia, yet brought up in this city at the feet of
Gamaliel, and taught according to the perfect manner of
the law of the fathers " (*Acts* 22.3). When he is on trial, it is
his claim : " I have lived in all good conscience before God
until this day . . . I am a Pharisee, the son of a Pharisee "
(*Acts* 23.1, 6).

Paul did not doubt that God had set so much of himself
in his world that all men had had the chance to know him
and were inexcusable if they remained in ignorance
(*Romans* 1.19, 20); but even when he has proved that the
Law cannot save men, and even when he has insisted that
the Gentiles have a law within their hearts, he can still cry
out : " What advantage then hath the Jew? or what profit
is there of circumcision?" And then he can answer :
" Much every way; chiefly, because unto them were committed the oracles of God " (*Romans* 3.1, 2).

Again and again there breathes through the thought of
Paul his pride and joy in the privilege of being a Jew, one of
the chosen people of God. Paul was the apostle to the
Gentiles, but it would be totally to misunderstand him to
think that he was ever hostile to the Jews. As Deissmann
finely points out : " Paul shows nothing of the renegade's
hatred." It often happens that when a man becomes a
renegade, a convert, a pervert—call him what you will—
he becomes bitter against that which he has left. It is true
that Paul had broken once and for all with Judaism, but at
heart he was still a Jew who would gladly have laid down
his life to bring fellow-Jews into the same faith as he himself had so gloriously discovered. Deissmann points out how
this Jewishness of Paul comes out again and again in the
everyday words and actions of Paul's life.

When Paul is dating things, it is in terms of Jewish dates and festivals that he always thinks. He writes to the Corinthians that he will stay at Ephesus until Pentecost (*I Corinthians* 16.8). In the narrative of the voyage to Rome, it is said that " sailing was now dangerous because the fast was now already past " (*Acts* 27.9). The fast in question was the Day of Atonement (*Leviticus* 23. 27-29) which fell in September, and in the ancient world sailing was considered unsafe between the months of September and March. The points of time from which Paul took all his dates were the great Jewish festivals and feasts.

Paul did not himself abandon the ancestral laws and customs of his own people; in many things he was still a devout Jew. Timothy's father was a Greek but his mother was a Jewess, and so we find Paul taking and circumcising Timothy in order that Timothy might be able to work amongst the Jews (*Acts* 16.3). The Nazirite vow was a vow which a devout Jew would take when he wished to express special gratitude to God. We find Paul himself taking that vow; we find that he had " shorn his head at Cenchrea; for he had a vow " (*Acts* 18.18). When Paul arrived in Jerusalem, we find him undertaking to be responsible for the expenses of certain men who were engaged in carrying out the Nazirite vow in order that he might make it clear that he was no destructive renegade from the Jewish faith (*Acts* 21.17-26).

Paul never forgot his Jewish origin; he never turned his back on the faith of his fathers; to Paul it was natural to say : " Unto the Jews I became as a Jew " (*I Corinthians* 9.20).

But it was not only in his words and actions that Paul's essential Jewishness came out; it was equally clear in his thoughts. Paul was a man of one book, and that book was the Old Testament. But there was this difference—when Paul quoted the Old Testament normally his quotations were not taken directly from the Hebrew; they were taken from the Septuagint, the Greek translation of the Old Testament, which Jews all over the world used.

Paul was brought up in a Greek city; all the wealth of

Greek literature lay open to him; yet at the most he only quotes a heathen writer twice. In *Acts* 17.28 he quotes the phrase, " We are also his offspring ", from Aratus, a Greek poet, and in *Titus* 1.12, the condemnation of the Cretans, " The Cretans are always liars, evil beasts, slow bellies ", is from a poet called Epimenides. Although all the wealth of Greek literature lay open before him, Paul's book was the Old Testament. Possibly it was not all he knew, but certainly it was all he needed.

When Paul uses the Old Testament, he uses it as a Jew would use it. Again and again he introduces an Old Testament quotation with the phrase : " It is written." That was the normal Greek legal phrase for a law or an agreement or a condition that was unalterable and inviolable. Paul's view of scripture as the voice of God was a Jewish view.

When Paul uses the Old Testament, he often allegorises it as a Jewish Rabbi would. For instance he takes the law of *Deuteronomy* 25.4 which says that the ox must not be muzzled when it is treading out the corn as an allegory of the fact that the Christian apostle and preacher must receive the material support of the Christian Church (*I Corinthians* 9.9). In *Galatians* 4.22-31 he works out a long allegory of the old and new covenants based on the story of Sarah and Hagar. In *I Corinthians* 10.4, he uses the rock from which the Israelites received water in the desert as an allegory of Jesus Christ. When Paul used scripture in that kind of way, he was using it in a way that any Jew would recognise, appreciate and understand.

Not only did Paul know the Old Testament as a devout Jew might know it; he was also a trained Rabbi and he knew the Old Testament as a Rabbi knew it. He knew not only the Old Testament; he also knew the special traditions of the Rabbis. He says in *Galatians* 3.19 that the Law was given through angels (cp. *Acts* 7.53; *Hebrews* 2.2). In the Old Testament itself there is no mention of angels in regard to the Law; in the old story, the Law was given direct by God to Moses. But as the years went on the sheer distance between God and man began to be stressed. Men began to be fascinated by what is called the transcendence of God.

They began to hold that God could never have had first-hand dealings with any man, not even with Moses, and that he must necessarily have used angels as his intermediaries; and so the Rabbinic tradition arose that the Law came to men from God by the mediation of angels. Paul knew that tradition and used it for his purposes.

Galatians 3.17 says that the Law was given 430 years after Abraham. That again is a Rabbinic addition to the Old Testament story. In *I Corinthians* 10.4 Paul speaks of "the rock that followed them". According to the traditions of the Rabbis the rock from which the children of Israel received water in their wilderness journeyings actually followed them throughout their journeyings ever after. That is a miracle story which is not part of the Old Testament narrative. It was one of the Rabbinic traditions and Paul knew it and used it.

If ever there was a Jew who was steeped in Judaism, that Jew was Paul. Let us before we leave the Jewish side of Paul look again at the claims he had to be the Jew *par excellence*. We have already cited his own list of Jewish qualifications as he gives it in *Philippians* 3.4-6. He was circumcised on the eighth day; that is to say, he bore in the body the badge and the mark that he was one of the chosen people, marked out by God as his own. He was of the race of Israel; that is to say, he was a member of the nation who stood in a covenant relationship with God, a relationship in which no other people stood. He was of the tribe of Benjamin. This is a claim which Paul reiterates in *Romans* 11.1. What is the point of this claim? The tribe of Benjamin has a unique place in the history of Israel. It was from Benjamin that the first king of Israel had come, for Saul was a Benjamite (*I Samuel* 9.1). When the tragic split of the kingdom came, Benjamin and Judah were the only two tribes who had stood true to Rehoboam (*I Kings* 12.21). Benjamin was the only one of the patriarchs who had actually been born in the land of promise. When Israel went into battle, it was the tribe of Benjamin which held the post of honour. The battle-cry of Israel was: "After thee, O Benjamin" (*Judges* 5.12; *Hosea* 5.8).

In lineage Paul was not only an Israelite; he was of the
aristocracy of Israel. He was a Hebrew of the Hebrews;
that is to say, Paul was not one of these Jews of the Dispersion who, in a foreign land, had forgotten their own tongue;
he was a Jew who still remembered and knew the language
of his fathers.

He was a Pharisee; that is to say, he was not only a devout Jew; he was more—he was one of "The Separated
Ones" who had foresworn all normal activities in order
to dedicate life to the keeping of the Law, and he had kept
it with such meticulous care that in the keeping of it he
was blameless.

No one could say that Paul had abandoned Judaism
because he did not understand it, or did not fully realise
what it was. No one could say that Paul had been driven
from Judaism because he had only experienced a truncated
or imperfect version of it. No one could say that Paul was
opposed to the principles of Jewish religion because he had
misunderstood them or knew them only from the outside.
Paul knew Judaism at its best and at its highest; he knew it
from the inside; he had gone through all the experiences,
both of height and of depth, that it could bring to any
man. Paul was the man ideally fitted to understand Christianity with all its Jewish background, and to bring Christianity to the Jews. There was one half of the world to
which Paul was, by his whole training and upbringing, the
ideal missionary.

But there was another half of world, the great Greek
world which lay far beyond the confines of Palestine and
the boundaries of Judaism. To the Jews it was easy for
Paul to become as a Jew, for he was a Jew. He must now
go on to see how he could also become a Greek to the
Greeks. We must now go on to see the other background of
this Paul who was so uniquely a man of two worlds.

II

THE MAN OF TWO WORLDS—
THE WORLD OF THE GREEK

We have seen the essential Jewishness of Paul; and we must
now turn to the other side of the picture. If there was one
thing of which Paul was certain it was that his unique privilege was to be the apostle to the Gentiles.

After Paul's conversion on the Damascus Road, word
from God came to the astonished Ananias that Paul was
coming to seek his help. Not unnaturally Ananias tended
to regard the one-time arch-persecutor of the Church with
a certain suspicion; but the voice of God came to him:
"He is a chosen vessel unto me, to bear my name before
the Gentiles" (*Acts* 9.15). From that time forward Paul
never lost an opportunity of insisting upon his apostleship
to the Gentiles. In his first recorded sermon, at Antioch in
Pisidia, when the Jews rejected the offer of the gospel, it is
the claim of Paul and Barnabas: "The Lord hath commanded us, saying, I have set thee to be a light of the
Gentiles" (*Acts* 13.47). When the Jews of the Synagogue of
Corinth showed themselves violently opposed to the Christian message, Paul's answer was: "From henceforth I will
go unto the Gentiles" (*Acts* 18.6). In his defence before
the infuriated mob at Jerusalem, Paul recalls how God's
voice had come to him after the stoning of Stephen: "De-
part: for I will send thee far hence unto the Gentiles"
(*Acts* 22.21). In his speech before King Agrippa, it is
Paul's claim that God had definitely commissioned him to
preach to the Gentiles (*Acts* 26.17, 23).

Again and again in his letters Paul discloses this same
special consciousness of being uniquely the messenger of
Christ to the Gentile world. He longs to come to Rome that
he may have some fruit there, as he has had among other
Gentiles (*Romans* 1.13). In the same letter he takes to him-

self the title of the apostle to the Gentiles, and calls himself the minister of Jesus Christ to the Gentiles (*Romans* 11.13; 15.16). In *Galatians* he says that the very purpose for which Christ was revealed in him was that he might preach him among the Gentiles (*Galatians* 1.16). And the same letter gives us a picture of a kind of agreement by which Peter went to the Jews and Paul to the Gentiles (*Galatians* 2.1-10). In the letter to the Ephesians Paul writes of himself as the prisoner of Christ for you Gentiles, and speaks of the grace that was given to him to preach to the Gentiles (*Ephesians* 3.1, 8). In the *Pastoral Epistles* Paul is described as a teacher of the Gentiles (*I Timothy* 2.7; *II Timothy* 1.11).

If ever a man was conscious of a destiny, that man was Paul, and the destiny was to bring the message of the good news to the Gentile world.

What special qualifications had Paul for this task? How did it come about that this member of the Jewish racial and intellectual aristocracy could be specially fitted to take Christianity to the Gentiles?

First of all, Paul was a citizen of Tarsus, and in that citizenship he took no small pride. When the military commander in Jerusalem was about to treat him like a common revolutionary, Paul stopped him with the imperious statement: " I am a man which am a Jew of Tarsus, . . . a citizen of no mean city " (*Acts* 21.39). When he addressed the hostile mob, he began by giving his credentials : " I am verily a man which am a Jew, born in Tarsus, a city in Cilicia." (*Acts* 22.3).

Tarsus was indeed no mean city. It was a city as far back as 860 B.C., for Shalmaneser of Assyria listed it among his conquests. Rather more than five hundred years later Tarsus saw Alexander the Great bathe in the icy waters of the River Cydnus, and catch a chill which nearly caused his death. Three hundred years later still, Tarsus was the dazzled spectator of one of Cleopatra's most famous exploits. Mark Antony was in Tarsus preparing for war against the distant Parthians on the far eastern borders of the Roman Republic. He suspected Cleopatra of plotting against him with his opponent Cassius, and he summoned her to appear before him. She appeared—in her own good time, and in her own flamboyant way.

Plutarch tells the story: "She received several letters both from Antony and his friends to summon her, but she took no account of these orders; but at last, as if in mockery of them, she came sailing up the River Cydnus in a barge with gilded stern and outstretched sails of purple, while oars of silver beat time to the music of flutes and fifes and harps. She herself lay all along under a canopy of gold, dressed as Venus in a picture, and beautiful young boys, like painted Cupids, stood on each side to fan her. Her maids were dressed like sea nymphs and graces, some steering at the rudder, some working at the ropes. The perfumes diffused themselves from the vessel to the shore which was covered with multitudes . . . The market-place was quite emptied and Antony at last was left alone sitting upon the tribunal, while word went through all the multitude that Venus was come to feast with Bacchus for the common good of Asia."

Shalmaneser, Alexander the Great, Antony and Cleopatra—truly Tarsus had seen the drama of history.

Tarsus was in the province of Cilicia, and it was one of the great centres at which the trade of the Mediterranean and of the hinterland of Asia Minor converged. It was specially famous for the manufacture of goats' hair felt, out of which tent-cloth, hangings, blankets, clothing, belts and saddles were made—and one of its greatest sons was a tent-maker.

Its greatness in trade was its own notable achievement. It lay on the River Cydnus. Two hundred feet wide, the river swept through the centre of the city. It lay ten miles inland from the mouth of the river. Half-way between Tarsus and the sea the river broadened out into a lake called Lake Rhegma. It was to that lake that Cleopatra came. The engineering skill and the commercial ambition of the Tarsians had lined three sides of that lake with harbours, docks and arsenals, and the ships of the Mediterranean sailed fully laden into, and out of, that harbour. In days when piracy was rampant the possession of a harbour in such a sheltered and easily defended position was a most priceless advantage.

But the Tarsians had performed an even greater feat than that. Thirty miles inland from Tarsus the huge Taurus range reared its bulk and its height; and there were few or no roads across it. But opening down into Tarsus there were the world famous Cilician Gates. There was a part of the range where a little stream came through a gorge which was little more than a cleft in the rock. Sometime in the dim and distant past, so long ago that the date was not even known, men from Tarsus had chiselled out of the rock of that narrow gorge, a carriage road beside the little river, and by that road the rich trade of the hinterland of Cappadocia and Galatia descended into Tarsus. Truly the Tarsians had succeeded in making their city great.

But not only was Tarsus a great commercial city; it was also a university town. Perhaps the university of Tarsus was not so academically distinguished as the universities of some of the older cities. But in one thing Tarsus surpassed them all, even Athens and Alexandria. It was a well-known fact that the enthusiasm for learning was greater in Tarsus than in any other city in the world. It never needed to import scholars; it had more than enough of its own. In fact, one of the most famous exports of Tarsus was scholars. Its young men went out to fill the chairs in other universities.

In particular, Tarsus was famous for philosophers, and especially for philosophers of the Stoic school. Strabo names five famous Stoics who were born in Tarsus—Antipater, Archedemus, Nestor, Athenodorus Cordylion (who was the friend and adviser of Augustus himself) and Athenodorus, the son of Sandon. In the nearby town of Soli, Chrysippus and Aratus, two of the greatest of all the Stoics, were born.

So much did Tarsus love and respect and admire learning that there was a time when Athenodorus and his fellow-philosophers not only taught their students but also governed the city. And in regard to government Tarsus was fortunate; either by luck or by good guidance it had always chosen the right side in the civil wars, and it had been rewarded with the status of a *civitas libera,* a free city, self-governing and independent.

Such was the place where Paul was born and brought up. It was a city so cosmopolitan that none could walk the streets without coming into contact with the ends of the earth. It was a city with such a history that none could live in it without some sense of greatness. It was a city with such a desire for knowledge, such a respect for scholarship, and such an intellectual ferment of thought that no thinking young man could entirely escape the contagion of the thronging ideas which crowded the air.

If a man was destined to be a missionary to the world at large, there was no better place in all the east for him to grow to manhood than in Tarsus. But Paul had an even more valuable qualification to be the apostle of the Gentiles, for he was a Roman citizen.

When Paul and Silas were thrown into gaol in Philippi and scourged without trial, the declaration, on the next day, of Paul's Roman citizenship brought from the local magistrates a terrified and abject apology (*Acts* 16.37-39). In Jerusalem the Roman military commander was compelled to arrest Paul to prevent a riot. They were about to bind Paul and to examine him under the lash, but Paul's declaration of his Roman citizenship halted the whole proceedings on the instant (*Acts* 22.24-30). When Paul was a prisoner at Cæsarea and, when he felt that any just trial was an impossibility, he made his appeal to Cæsar, and, because he was a Roman citizen, none could deny his request (*Acts* 25.9-12).

Roman citizenship was no empty honour, and no formal dignity. The Roman law was clear : a Roman citizen could not be bound and could not be scourged; a Roman citizen could not be crucified. "It is a breach of the law for a Roman citizen to be bound; it is a crime for him to be beaten," said Cicero. If a man claimed Roman citizenship, no matter where he was, to the ends of the earth, the might and majesty of Rome was behind him. "How often," said

Cicero, "has this exclamation, 'I am a Roman citizen,' brought aid and safety even among barbarians in the remotest parts of the earth!"

Paul was proud of his Roman citizenship. In Philippi he insisted on a public apology from the local magistrates before he would even consent to emerge from the prison into which they had wrongly thrown him (*Acts* 16.37). When the military commander at Jerusalem commented that he himself had bought the citizenship at a great price, Paul proudly answered: "I was free born" (*Acts* 22.28).

Not only was Paul proud of his citizenship; he was proud of the Roman Empire. When he wrote to the Christians at Rome, he bade them be subject to the powers that be, for these powers had been given their authority by God (*Romans* 13.1-5). In the *Pastoral Epistles* the duty of praying for the Emperor is laid upon the Church (*I Timothy* 2.1-3). *II Thessalonians* 2.6, 7 is a rather puzzling passage. In that passage the thought is that in this world there is a power which is restraining the swelling insolence of evil; and to Paul that power was Rome.

In the ancient world the Roman citizenship was an accolade of honour and a safe-conduct to the ends of the earth. Paul possessed that citizenship, and he was proud of it. It will be interesting to surmise how Paul's family received that citizenship.

There were two kinds of Roman citizenship. There was that which conferred *commercium,* trading rights, and that which conferred not only *commercium,* but also *connubium,* marriage rights. And it is clear that it was full citizenship which Paul enjoyed.

We may begin with certain things which we may regard as facts. Paul was born in Tarsus (*Acts* 22.3); and Paul's father, like Paul himself, was a Pharisee (*Acts* 23.6). It is in the last degree unlikely that a man who was a Pharisee would willingly live out of the land of Palestine. We cannot think that at some time Paul's father had emigrated to Cilicia in search of fame and fortune; a Pharisee would never willingly have lived away from the sacred soil of the

Holy Land; it must have been some stern necessity which brought him there.

Further, Roman citizenship could be acquired in several ways. It could be purchased, although not everyone would be accepted as a suitable purchaser. It was by purchase that the Roman military commander in Jerusalem had acquired his citizenship (*Acts* 22.28). It is quite certain that no Pharisee would ever go out of his way to purchase Roman citizenship. It was not that the Pharisees were hostile to Rome; they were in fact willing to live under any government which would allow them to live in accordance with the Law; but a Pharisee would have been totally uninterested in becoming a Roman citizen.

The citizenship could be granted to chosen people for distinguished services to the Roman state, especially in time of crisis and of need. It was given to Roman soldiers when they had completed twenty-four years' service. It is hardly likely that the citizenship came to Paul's family in either of these ways.

Sometimes, in reward for some act of fidelity or as a special mark of favour, the citizenship was given to the whole population of certain towns or areas—and it may well be that it was in this way that Paul's family first received the citizenship. Let us see if we can trace any way in which that might have happened.

Jerome passes on to us a tradition regarding Paul's family. He gives it in two forms. " Paul was of the tribe of Benjamin, and from a town in Judæa called Gischala. When this town was captured by the Romans, he migrated with his parents to Tarsus in Cilicia, and by them he was sent to Jerusalem for the study of the law, and was there trained by Gamaliel, a most learned man."

The second form is : " We have received a story like this. They say that the parents of the apostle Paul came from the district of Gischala in Judæa, and that, when the whole province was laid waste by the hand of Rome, and when the Jews were dispersed throughout the world, they were transferred to Tarsus, a city in Cilicia, and that Paul, who was at that time a mere lad, accompanied his parents."

Wherever Jerome got that story, it cannot be true. We have Paul's own word for it that he was born in Tarsus and not in Gischala. Gischala was in Galilee; it was the last city to capitulate in the last terrible days when the Romans finally broke the Jews, but that was in A.D. 67. True, there was savage fighting near Gischala in 4 B.C. in the troubles that followed the death of Herod. But, no matter how we try to explain it, Jerome's story does not seem to fit the facts.

David Smith felt that Paul's citizenship might be explained in this way. In 63 B.C. Pompey invaded and captured Jerusalem. At that time he carried thousands of Jews back to Rome as slaves. In due time these Jews settled down in Rome and prospered. They ultimately came to possess a part of the city as their own; and when in 4 B.C. a Jewish embassy came to Rome, it was greeted by no fewer than 8,000 Jews who were resident in Rome. Many of these Jews became citizens. Julius Cæsar, for instance, had been specially kind to the Jews, and as Suetonius the historian tells us, when Julius Cæsar died, " a throng of foreigners went about lamenting each after the fashion of his country, above all the Jews." It might be that Paul's father or grandfather had been among those carried off to Rome, had acquired the citizenship, and later come to Tarsus.

There is still another suggestion. About the year 175 B.C. great changes happened in Tarsus. At that time Antiochus Epiphanes refounded and reorganised the city. In the reorganisation citizenship was thrown open to the Jews, for they were useful and often wealthy citizens, and many Jewish families either migrated or were transported to Tarsus at that time. It is by far the most likely thing that Paul's ancestors came to Tarsus then. That move would make them citizens of Tarsus, but not yet of Rome. Thereafter, there were times when Tarsus had the closest possible connection with Rome. In 64 B.C. it was the headquarters of Pompey, the great Roman general who purged the seas of pirates and the roads of brigands and who brought peace to Asia Minor. No doubt many received the citizenship under him. In 47 B.C. Julius Cæsar came to Tarsus on his eastern campaigns, and so enthusiastic were the Tarsians in his support that they changed the name of their city to Juliopolis, although the new name did not last. Certainly many Tarsians would have received the citizenship then. In 42 B.C. Mark Antony had his headquarters in Tarsus; and again the citizenship would have been conferred on many, although Mark Antony, who needed money, would be more likely to sell the citizenship than to gift it. Finally in 31 B.C. Augustus conferred many benefits on Tarsus in gratitude for her fidelity to his cause. It may well have been at one of these times that Paul's family first received citizenship.

Here indeed we have something of significance. If it be true—and as it may well be true—that behind Paul there lay generations of family residence in Tarsus, then Paul grew up in an atmosphere in which he was as familiar with Greek and Roman thought as he was with the Jewish thought of his own nation.

In order that Christianity might go out to all the world a unique person was necessary—and Paul was that person. Here uniquely was the man of two worlds, the man who was Jewish to the last fibre of his being, but also the man who knew the Romans and the Greeks as few Jews knew them. Here indeed was the man prepared by God to be the bridge between two worlds, and to be the bridge by which the Gentiles might come to God.

III

PAUL'S THINKING ABOUT GOD

We have seen the background out of which Paul grew. Now we go on to look at his actual thought and teaching, and we begin with Paul's thinking about God.

Every Jewish Synagogue service began, and still begins, with the recital of the Shema, and the great basic sentence of the Shema is: "Hear, O Israel: the Lord our God is one Lord" (*Deuteronomy* 6.4). In that sentence there is laid down an uncompromising monotheism. In a world which believed in many gods the Jews believed in one God, and that for Paul, too, is the beginning of his thinking about God.

He writes to his people at Corinth: "There is none other God but one . . . To us there is but one God" (*I Corinthians* 8.4, 6). The belief in the one true God may be said to be the foundation stone of all Paul's thinking.

But there is another great dominant thought in all Paul's teaching. This God who is the one God is also God the Father. There is not one single letter that he ever wrote in which Paul does not call God *Father* (*I Thessalonians* 1.1; *II Thessalonians* 1.2; *Galatians* 1.3; *I Corinthians* 1.3; *II Corinthians* 1.2; *Romans* 1.7; *Ephesians* 1.2; *Colossians* 1.2; *Philippians* 1.2; *Philemon* 3).

Now these two great foundation beliefs of Paul complete and complement each other. If Paul were to say that there is one God, and leave it at that, the might and majesty and power of the lonely God would be secured and safeguarded. If Paul were to say that God is Father, the benevolence and the love and the goodwill of God would be stressed. The first statement, the statement of what we might call God's onlyness, assures us of God's power, but says nothing of any interest he may have in men. The second statement assures us of God's kindliness, but gives us no guarantee that the kindliness may not be frustrated and hindered. But when the two ideas are put together, we get the full, rounded idea of God, as a God whose power is always motivated by his love, and whose love is always backed by his power. So Paul sums it up: " To us there is but one God, the Father " (*I Corinthians* 8.6); and in that single phrase he gives us the Christian assurance of a God whose power will never be used except in love, and a God whose loving purposes because of his power can never be frustrated.

To Paul, this God and Father was also Creator. "All things," he said, "are of God" (*I Corinthians* 11.12). "Of him and through him and to him are all things" (*Romans* 11.36). With this idea of God the Creator, Paul joins the idea of the Son as God's instrument, and agent in creation, just as John was later to do in an even fuller way. Paul speaks of " one Lord Jesus by whom are all things " (*I Corinthians* 8.6). He speaks of God who created all things by Jesus Christ (*Ephesians* 3.9). " By him," he says, " all things were created" (*Colossians* 1.16). This is the doctrine which John states so definitely in the prologue to his gospel when he says : " All things were made by him and without him was not anything made that was made " (*John* 1.3).

It may seem strange to us that Paul makes so much of God as creator, and of the Son's part in the work of creation. But he did so in answer to an increasing tendency of thought in the ancient world. This tendency was later to become known by the name Gnosticism, and since much of the New Testament is written against a background of Gnosticism, and is written to counteract Gnostic tendencies, it is as well to see here at the beginning what Gnosticism was.

Gnosticism was an attempt to solve the problem of sin and suffering in this world. The Gnostics believed that spirit is essentially good, and that matter is essentially evil. They further believed that the creation of the world was out of matter which already existed, and that this matter was essentially flawed. If we may put it so, the whole trouble about the world is that it is made and fashioned out of faulty material. The stuff of which the world is formed is evil. The Gnostic went on to say that, since God is pure spirit and altogether good, he could not possibly himself have touched and handled and fashioned this flawed matter. So, in order to touch matter, God put out a series of emanations, or æons, as they called them. Each succeeding emanation was a little farther away from God, until at the end of this long line and series there was an emanation so distant from God that it could touch and handle matter. It was this emanation which actually created the world.

The Gnostics went further. As the emanations grew farther and farther from God, they knew less and less about God. At some part in the series, an emanation is arrived at who is entirely ignorant of God. Then still lower down in the series the emanations become not only ignorant of but actively hostile to God. And so in the end the Gnostics came to believe that the world was created by a creator God who was ignorant of and hostile to the true God.

The final step in Gnostic thought was to hold that this ignorant, hostile, creating God was to be identified with the God of the Old Testament; and the real God, who was pure spirit and remote from the work of creation, was to be identified with the true God, the God whom Jesus came to make known to men.

This line of thought became increasingly common in the ancient world. The ancient world was haunted by the thought of the evil matter. That is why so many of the New Testament writers stress the fact that God is Creator, and that God's instrument in creation is not some distant, ignorant, hostile æon, but his Son and his Word. The Gnostic believed that we live in an evil world; the Christian believes that God made all things and made them well.

But Paul also believed that God's act of creation was also an act of self-revelation. To put it in a modern way, Paul believed that God put so much of himself into the world that by studying the world men ought to be able to arrive at God. That is the meaning of the famous passage in *Romans* 1.19-21. "For the invisible things of him from the creation of the world are clearly seen, being understood by the things that are made, even his eternal power and god-head; so that they are without excuse." It was Paul's belief that God's act of creation was an act of self-revelation; that this world was the garment of the living God; that if men had the eyes to see and the heart to understand they could see God everywhere in the world which he made.

A great artist tells that it was his father who taught him to see and to love beauty. His father used to take him out in the evening time, and the father and son would lie in the long grass beside the wood. They would watch the rabbits play, and the birds swoop by, and the corn field rippling like the waves of the sea beneath the wind. One evening there was a sunset of surpassing majesty and splendour, and at the sight of it his father stood up, removed his cap and looked at the splendour of the dying sun, and said : " My son, it is God." Paul would have wished every man to see and to make that act of instinctive reverence.

Paul believed that God's interest in the world did not end with the work of creation. He believed that God was still the sustaining God, whose work of creation was still going on. He saw that continued activity of God in the processes of the natural world. "Neither is he that planteth any-thing," he said, " neither he that watereth; but God that giveth the increase " (*I Corinthians* 3.7). Paul had dis-covered the truth that must continually be rediscovered. Man can do many things. He can change things, and alter them, and modify them, and rearrange them. But he can-not create them. Man controls many forces, but man does not control the force of life, and he cannot make a living thing. Creation is the prerogative of God; the secret of life is with God. Paul never thought of a God, who, as it were, wound things up and set them going, and then left them to themselves. He thought of a God always and continually active and at work in the universe which he had made. Creation and providence both belong to God.

So far we have been seeing God as it were in world affairs. Now we must go on to see how Paul thought of God, not only as active in the world, but active in his own life.

Paul saw God's hand in his own spiritual pilgrimage. He saw his life as something planned and designed by God. He speaks of God "who separated me from my mother's womb" (*Galatians* 1.15). He speaks of God "separating him unto the gospel" (*Romans* 1.1). Paul thought of himself as a man set apart by God for a special purpose even before he was born. He sees his apostleship not as something to which he attained, not as something to which he was called by men, but as something which came to him by plan and design of God. "Paul, an apostle of Jesus Christ," he says, "by the will of God" (*II Corinthians* 1.1). Even more fully he sets it out at the beginning of Galatians: "Paul, an apostle, not of men, neither by man, but by Jesus Christ and God the Father" (*Galatians* 1.1). Paul saw God, not only in the great lines of world creation and world history but also in his own life. Paul would have agreed with the man who said that every man is a dream of God.

Paul went even farther than that. He did not see God only in the great events and the crucial moments on which his life had hinged. He saw God in the life of everyday. When he writes to the Corinthians he tells them: "I will come to you shortly, if the Lord will" (*I Corinthians* 4.19). When he writes to the Roman Church he tells that he prays, "If by any means now at length I might have a prosperous journey, by the will of God, to come unto you" (*Romans* 1.10). To Paul the God who created the world was never too busy to be bothered with his own life.

Another way of putting this would be to say that to Paul God was a supplying God. This God, who created men, and who directed their lives, did not leave men to carry out his commandments unaided and to go upon his tasks unassisted. With the need came the power; with the task came the ability to do it. "Not that we are sufficient of ourselves," said Paul, "but our sufficiency is of God" (*II Corinthians* 3.5).

In the midst of his troubles, when life was an almost intolerable burden, he heard God say: "My grace is sufficient for you; for my strength is made perfect in weakness" (*II Corinthians* 12.9). Even when he was in prison in

Rome he writes to his friends in Philippi : " My God shall supply all your needs " (*Philippians* 4.9). John Buchan described an atheist as a man who has no invisible means of support. To Paul a Christian was a man who had the continual support of God.

The relationship between God and Jesus is something to which we shall have again and again to return. But at the moment we must note that God was behind every single act of the life of Jesus.

God was behind the Incarnation. God was behind the coming of Jesus into the world. His coming into the world was not, as it were, something which the Son suggested. It is God who is the prime mover and who is behind it all. So Paul speaks of God sending his Son in the likeness of sinful flesh (*Romans* 8.3). He says that " when the fulness of time was come God sent forth his Son " (*Galatians* 4.4). To Paul, in the fullest sense of the term, the coming of Jesus into the world was an act of God.

God was behind the Cross. The Cross was not an independent act of Jesus. The Cross was not solely the result of the fury and the sin of men. The Cross was an event within the plan and the purpose of God. " Jesus," says Paul, " who was delivered for our offences " (*Romans* 4.25). " Jesus," says Paul, " who gave himself for our sins, according to the will of God " (*Galatians* 1.4). " He that spared not his own Son," says Paul, " but delivered him up for us all " (*Romans* 8.32). It is none other than God who is behind the coming of Jesus into the world, and the sacrifice of the life of Jesus upon the Cross.

God was behind the Resurrection. Here indeed is one of the most familiar thoughts of Paul, a thought to be found in every epistle. In *Galatians* 1.1 Paul speaks of " Jesus Christ, and God the Father, who raised him from the dead ". In *Romans* 4.24 he speaks of " him that raised up Jesus our Lord from the dead ". God is behind both our quickening from sin and its death and the raising of Jesus from the death of the Cross. " God hath quickened us together with Christ," he writes (*Ephesians* 2.5). " You," he writes, " being dead in your sins hath he quickened with him " (*Colossians* 2.13). The Resurrection was to Paul, not so much an achievement of Jesus, as an act of God.

For Paul, God was behind the Incarnation, the Cross and the Resurrection. Here is something which we shall have to recall to our minds again and again. There is a way of presenting the gospel which comes perilously near to blasphemy, a way in which Paul's gospel especially is wrongly presented. Sometimes the gospel is presented as if there was a contrast between a stern and angry God and a gentle and loving Christ, as if there was a contrast between a God who was the judge of the souls of men and a Christ who was the lover of the souls of men, a contrast between a God who wished to condemn and a Christ who wished to save. Sometimes the gospel is presented in such a way that it sounds as if Jesus Christ had done something to change the attitude of God, as if he had changed God's wrath to love, as if he had persuaded God's uplifted hand not to strike the contemplated blow. Nothing could be further from the truth, and nothing could be a graver distortion of the gospel of Paul. As John saw so clearly, it was because God so loved the world that he sent his Son into the world (*John* 3.16). As Paul saw so vividly, it was God who was behind the whole process of redemption. It is God's love, God's desire to save which dominates the whole scene. The initiative is the initiative of God. Behind every act of Jesus is God. Jesus to Paul was not the pacifier of the wrath of God; he was the bringer of the love of God. And now we must go on to study that divine initiative in fuller detail.

IV

THE DIVINE INITIATIVE

Simone Weil has said: "One might lay down as a postulate: All conceptions of God which are incompatible with a movement of pure charity are false. All other conceptions of him, in varying degree are true." There is a way of presenting Paul's gospel which is incompatible with the pure charity of God. Sometimes Paul's gospel is preached in such a way that God and Jesus Christ are set over against each other and contrasted with each other. The love and the grace and the mercy of Jesus Christ are set over against the wrath and the austerity and the judgment of God. The implication is that through something that Jesus did the attitude of God to men was changed, that God was persuaded and pacified by Jesus Christ into changing his condemnation into forgiveness.

The more we study Paul's own writings, the more we see that any such conception is the reverse of the truth as Paul saw it. If one thing is clear, it is that, to Paul, the whole initiative of the process of salvation lies with God.

The will behind the whole process of salvation is the will of God. Paul writes to the Corinthians, "He who stablishes us with you in Christ, and hath anointed us, is God" (*II Corinthians* 1.21). He speaks to the Thessalonians of "the will of God in Christ Jesus" (*I Thessalonians* 5.18). He writes to the Galatians of "Jesus who gave himself for our sins, according to the will of God" (*Galatians* 1.4).

So far from God's attitude being changed by anything that Jesus did, it was precisely God's attitude to men that Jesus expressed. So far from God's purpose being deflected by anything that Jesus did, it was precisely the purpose of God that Jesus came to fulfil. Salvation did not come to men in opposition to the will of God; it came because it was the will of God.

It was the love of God which was behind the whole process of salvation. Paul writes to the Thessalonians that it is
" our Lord Jesus Christ himself, and God, even our Father,
who has loved us, and has given us everlasting consolation "
(*II Thessalonians* 2.16). It was his love that God com-
mended to us in the death of Christ (*Romans* 5.8). It is the
goodness of God which leads men to repentance (*Romans*
2.4). It is from the love of God that nothing can separate
us (*Romans* 8.39). It is by God's mercies that Paul appeals
to men (*Romans* 12.1). He writes to the Ephesians of God
" who is rich in mercy, because of the great love wherewith
he loved us " (*Ephesians* 2.4). It is the Father himself who
has made us " fit to be partakers of the inheritance of the
saints in light " (*Colossians* 1.12). Jesus Christ came to tell
men, not that God hates sinners, but that he loves them. It
is the simple fact that no one ever wrote with such lyrical
splendour of the love of God as Paul did. Even to suggest
that Paul contrasted the love of Christ and the wrath of
God is to make a travesty of his gospel.

It is God who is behind the initiative of reconciliation.
In that great passage in *II Corinthians* 5.18-20 three times
in as many verses the initiative in reconciliation is referred
to God. It is God who has reconciled us to himself in Jesus
Christ. God was in Christ reconciling the world unto himself. And the final appeal is : " Be ye reconciled to God."

In *Romans* 5.10 it is we who are reconciled to God. In
Colossians 1.20 it is God, who is making peace by the blood
of the Cross, and reconciling all things unto himself. In all
Paul's writings God is never spoken of as being reconciled to
man, for the simple reason that any such reconciliation is
totally unnecessary. Always the one thing necessary is that
man should be reconciled to God. The responsibility for the
breach between man and God lies, not with God, but with
man. It was man's attitude to God which needed to be
changed. God's attitude to man always was and always
must be patient love, unwearied forgiveness, and undefeatable seeking.

Paul can speak quite indiscriminately about the Gospel
of Jesus Christ and the Gospel of God. The very essence of

Paul's preaching was good news about God brought to men by Jesus Christ. He tells the Thessalonians that " we were bold in our God to speak unto you the gospel of God " (*I Thessalonians* 2.2). He tells them that he preached to them the gospel of God (*I Thessalonians* 2.8, 9). Yet in the very same letter he can speak of Timothy our fellow-labourer in the gospel of Christ (*I Thessalonians* 3.2). He speaks of himself as being separated unto the gospel of God (*Romans* 1.1). Jesus did not come to introduce to the world a new-made gospel as a substitute for news of the wrath of God. It was precisely good news about the love of God that Jesus came to bring.

Whenever Paul speaks about the grace of God, his habit is to associate God and Jesus Christ in this matter of grace. Nothing could be further from the thought of Paul than to think that all the grace was of Jesus and all the stern justice was of God. The grace which Jesus brings to men is nothing other than the grace of God. It is that very grace of God which was in Jesus Christ. When he writes to the Thessalonians, he speaks of " the grace of our God and the Lord Jesus Christ " (*II Thessalonians* 1.12). He greets the Galatians with " grace and peace from God the Father and from our Lord Jesus Christ " (*Galatians* 1.3). He speaks to the Corinthians of " the grace of God which is given you by Jesus Christ " (*I Corinthians* 1.4).

The grace behind the whole process of salvation is the grace of God. Jesus neither discovered nor created grace; he brought to men the already existing grace of God.

It was God who sent Jesus Christ into this world. It is not that Jesus, as it were, said : " I will take the initiative and will go into the world and make my sacrifice and lay down my life, if perchance it may pacify my Father's anger and free men from the wrath to come." If we may put it so, it was that God laid upon Jesus the task of providing the way to salvation, which was already his only aim.

Paul tells the Galatians that God sent his Son in the ful-ness of time (*Galatians* 4.4). He tells the Corinthians that it is God who made Jesus Christ to be sin for the sake of men (*II Corinthians* 5.21). Jesus is the unspeakable gift of God

(*II Corinthians* 9.15). The gift of eternal life is the gift of
God (*Romans* 6.23). God sent his Son into the world in flesh
which was exactly like our own (*Romans* 8.3). It is Paul's
supreme proof of the lengths to which the love of God will
go that God who spared not his own Son will surely go to
any lengths in his love and care for men (*Romans* 8.32).
The fact that Jesus came into the world at all is due to nothing else than the seeking love of God.

It has so often happened that a distorted version of
Paul's gospel has been preached and taught to men, and
the disastrous result of that distortion has been that men
have so often had a division in their minds between God
and Jesus. They have come to look on God as a person to
be feared and Jesus as a person to be loved. They have
felt at home with Jesus, but strange and uncomfortable and
scared of God. They have looked on Jesus as their defence
and rescuer from the wrath of God. So deeply is that ingrained into the minds of some people in their younger days
that they never wholly grow out of it. They feel that Jesus
is indeed their friend, but they are haunted rather than
helped by the very thought of God.

In John we come upon that immortal sentence : "He
that hath seen me hath seen the Father" (*John* 14.9). The
tragedy is that to so many people God is the opposite of
Jesus; but the whole teaching of the New Testament, and
above all the teaching of Paul, is that when we look on the
seeking love, the unwearied forgiveness, the infinite compassion, the yearning gentleness of Jesus, we are looking at
the heart of God, fully displayed as nowhere else in all the
world.

Jesus did not come to save men against the will of God;
he came to bring men the good news that God wanted
nothing so much as that men should come home to himself
in contrite love and trust.

V

THE CALL OF GOD

We have seen how Paul believed with his whole heart that God was behind the whole process of salvation. The initiative in salvation is a divine initiative, the initiative of God.

But to Paul the matter was even more personal than that. If we say that it is the will of God that is behind the whole process of salvation, and if we leave it at that, we might feel that the whole purpose of God was a kind of generalised purpose aiming at the salvation of mankind. But Paul was sure that the purpose of God was not a generalised but an individualised purpose, that God's purpose was not so much the salvation of mankind, but the salvation of each individual man. As Augustine put it in the famous sentence with which Paul would have wholeheartedly agreed : " God loves each one of us as if there was only one of us to love." For that reason Paul makes a great deal of the call of God.

The call of God is not simply a wide, general call to all mankind; it is God's personal summons and invitation to each individual man. God does not only purpose the salvation of all mankind, he has " his own secret stairway into every heart ". He invites each man individually to respond to him.

The idea of the call of God runs through all Paul's letters; and it is of the greatest interest and the greatest significance to see to what Paul believed God is calling men.

Paul believed that God is calling men to salvation. He writes to the Thessalonians that God is calling them, not to wrath, but to obtain salvation (*I Thessalonians* 5.9). God has from the beginning chosen them to salvation (*II Thessalonians* 2.13). It is God's aim to rescue men from the hopeless situation in which they find themselves, and to

liberate them from the chains in which they have involved
themselves.

The ancient world felt pessimistically that it had lost the
moral battle. " Men," said Epictetus, " were sorely conscious of their weakness in necessary things." " Men love
their vices and hate them at the same time," said Seneca.
" It is not only that we have acted amiss," he said. " We
shall do so to the end." Persius, the Roman poet, wrote
despairingly : " Let the guilty see virtue and pine that they
have lost her for ever." He spoke about " filthy Natta be-
numbed by vice ". " When a man," said Epictetus, " is
hardened like a stone, how can any argument deal with
him?" Seneca declared that what men needed above all
was " a hand let down to lift them up ". The ancient world
was deeply conscious that it was inextricably entangled and
enmeshed in sin. It felt helpless in this world, and under
certain judgment in the next. In such a situation God
called men to accept the deliverance, the rescue, the redemption, the salvation that he was offering men through
Jesus Christ.

Paul believed that God was calling men to holiness. He
tells the Thessalonians that God calls them to a holy life (*I
Thessalonians* 4.7). The root meaning of the word holy
(*hagios*) is *different*. To be holy is to be different; it is to
have a different standard, a different peace and beauty from
the stained, frustrated, defeated life of the world. God calls
men to a life in which there has opened out the possibility
of a new victory over sin and a new loveliness and beauty.

Paul believed that God was calling men to peace. He
tells the Corinthians that they are called, not to bondage,
but to peace (*I Corinthians* 7.15). Wherein lay this peace?
The ancient world could never get beyond a belief in the
blind tyranny, the utter indifference of the sheer capricious-
ness of the gods. Man was what Homer long ago called
the *paignion theōn*, the plaything of the gods. How could
man know peace if he forever trembled at the thought of
the eternal judge? How could he know peace if he believed
that he lived in a world which did not care? How could he
know peace if he felt that he was caught up in a blind fate

and an iron determinism which would crush the life out of him? How could he know peace if he felt that he was the helpless plaything of the immortal gods? But peace comes when a man realises that the sum total of things is under the direction of one whose name is Father and whose heart is love. The call of God is a summons to men to find the peace of realising that the world is their Father's house.

Paul believed that God's call was a call to grace. He tells the Galatians that God calls them to the grace of Christ (*Galatians* 1.6). The basic meaning of grace is something which is freely and undeservedly given in the sheer generosity of God. Grace is something which a man could never deserve and never earn, but which is given to him in the outgoing love of God.

Here indeed was something new. Until this time men had seen God in terms of law. God had laid down certain laws. The dilemma was that these laws must be kept, but could never be kept. They were both obligatory and impossible. Man was for ever in default. But now in Christ God calls to men to realise that they cannot earn, but can only accept in wonder, his rescuing and redeeming love. The minute a man realises that, the tension of life is gone.

Paul believed that God's call was a call to fellowship with Christ. He tells the Corinthians that God has called them into the fellowship of Jesus Christ (*I Corinthians* 1.9). The supreme horror of life is loneliness; and the supreme value of life is friendship.

In one of the Socratic dialogues a simple soul who had been admitted to that great fellowship which gathered around Socrates, was asked to name the boon in life for which he was most grateful. His answer was : " That being such as I am, I have the friends I have." The call of God is to share the greatest friendship in the world, the friendship of Jesus Christ.

Paul believed that the call of God was a call to share the kingdom and the glory of his Son. He tells the Thessalonians that God has called them to his kingdom and his glory (*I Thessalonians* 2.12). The invitation of God is the invitation to share in the present power and the future

triumph of Jesus Christ. Even in days of persecution, even
in days when the world seems to be winning, it is the man
who has accepted the invitation of God who is ultimately on
the winning side.

Paul believed that that call of God was a call which had
been sounding out from all eternity. He writes to the
Ephesians that they were chosen before the foundation of
the world (*Ephesians* 1.4). Sometimes the Cross is depicted
as if it were a kind of emergency measure of God, as if he
had tried the Cross when all other things had failed. It is
the belief of Paul that through all eternity God has been
loving his men; that through all eternity man's sin has
been breaking his heart; that through all eternity God's
love has been sacrificing and suffering and seeking for men.

It is as if the Cross was a window opening for one
moment of time upon the eternal suffering love of the heart
of God. In one of Ibsen's plays there is a passage like this
about Christ : " Where is he now? Has he been at work
elsewhere since that happened at Golgotha? . . . Where is
he now? What if that at Golgotha, near Jerusalem, was but
a wayside matter, a thing done, as it were, in the passing?
What if he goes on and on, and suffers and dies and con-
quers again and again from world to world?" That may be
a startling way to put the matter. But the fact remains that
the Cross is the sign and symbol in a moment of time of the
sacrificing love which has been in the heart of God from
the foundation of the world.

Paul believed that the call of God came to men supremely
in Christ. He writes to the Roman Christians that they are
among those who are called by Jesus Christ (*Romans* 1.6).
All through the ages God has been sending his call to men,
by the voice of conscience, by the experiences of life, by
the voices of the prophets, by the events of history. These
things men might be too blind to see, and too dull to
appreciate, but in Jesus Christ there comes the supreme call,
so plain that none can fail to hear it.

Paul believed that God's call came by the preaching of
the gospel. He writes to the Thessalonians that God had
called them by the gospel which he had preached (*II Thes-*

salonians 2.14). Two things emerge from that. First, the call was the call of the *gospel*. The call was not the call of a threat; it was the call of good news. It was not the summons to avoid damnation; it was the invitation to accept love.

Second, it came to men by preaching. Men must be confronted with the call and the invitation of God. It is the task of every Christian, it is the task of the Church, and it is supremely the task of the preacher to bring to men who have never heard it, or who refuse to listen to it, the call of God.

VI

PAUL'S THINKING ABOUT JESUS CHRIST

When we try to find out what Paul thought and believed
about Jesus Christ, we must begin by remembering two
things. First, Paul was not a systematic theologian. Paul
was not in the least like a man sitting in a library or in a
study carefully and logically compiling a system of theology. First and foremost Paul argued from experience.
When he talks about Jesus, he is not offering us something
which is the fruit of thought and deduction and study and
the careful balancing of one theory against another theory
and one philosophy against another philosophy. He is continually saying: "This is what happened to me. This is
what I have experienced. This is what Jesus did for me.
This I know to be true."

It is quite true that it may be a quite unfair distinction
to make. But it is true to say that Paul's interest was not in
theology, but in religion. He was never concerned to draw
up and work out a system which would be fully satisfactory
to the mind and intellect: he was concerned to tell men of
an experience-based faith, by which they might live. When
Paul speaks of Jesus, he is simply setting down his own
experience of his risen Lord.

Second, we must remember that there was nothing static
about Paul's belief. Paul was for ever faced with the ever
moving and changing stream of human experience. He
was for ever involved in changing situations. He had to
meet one error after another; he had to match himself with
one set of thinkers after another; he had to deal with one
heresy after another. He was living in days when the
Church was still in a ferment, days long before the time
when the Church had settled down to an institutional
orthodoxy. And to meet each changing situation and
problem he had to draw new truth and new treasures out

of what he himself called the unsearchable riches of Christ.
He was ever discovering new greatnesses and new ade-
quacies in Christ. No matter how long Paul had lived he
would never have arrived at a static religion.

It is said that a certain famous lady was asked what
quality she regarded as most necessary for a person to
possess in order that he might excel in life. She answered in
one word : "Adaptability." In the highest possible sense,
and not in any time-serving sense, Paul's theology was an
adaptable theology. It was always deepening and develop-
ing and widening to meet the new situations which the life
of the growing Church brought to him. That is why it is
not possible to make a neat pattern of Paul's thinking about
Jesus, for as the years went on Jesus became ever more
wonderful to Paul.

We must begin somewhere, and we begin with that
which is most basic. With the exception of *II Thessalonians* and *Philemon,* there is not one single letter in which
Paul does not refer to Jesus as the Son of God. In every
other letter, either by direct statement or by unmistakable
implication, we meet that conception which for Paul was
the starting point of all things.

And it is to be noted that again and again this statement
that Jesus is the Son of God occurs at the very beginning
of Paul's letters as if by it he struck what was for him the
keynote of the christian gospel (cp. *I Thessalonians* 1.10;
Galatians 1.16; 2.20; 4.4; *I Corinthians* 1.9; *II Corinthians*
1.19; 1.3; *Romans* 1.3; 1.9; 8.32; *Ephesians* 1.3; *Colossians*
1.3). First and foremost Paul believed and insisted that
Jesus stood in a unique relationship with God.

And yet there is something else to be set beside that.
Never at any time did Paul identify Jesus Christ and God.
He never equated Jesus Christ and God. He may and does
equate the love and the gospel and the grace and the work
of Jesus Christ and of God, but never does he as we might
put it, personally identify Jesus and God.

Nowhere does Paul reach greater heights in his conception of Jesus than in the letter to the Colossians, where he
goes the length of saying that Jesus is the fulness of the

godhead bodily (*Colossians* 2.9) yet even in that letter he has the picture of Jesus at the right hand of God (*Colossians* 3.1). We have no wish to take a phrase like that with a crude literalism, yet it remains true that no one could even use it unless he had a clear distinction in his mind between Jesus Christ and God.

Paul goes even further than that. There is a sense for Paul in which Jesus is subordinate to God. He writes to the Corinthians : " But I would have you know, that the head of every man is Christ . . . and the head of Christ is God " (*I Corinthians* 11.3). In his picture of the end of things, he writes to the Corinthians : " And when all things shall be subdued unto him, then shall the Son also be subject unto him, that put all things under him, that God may be all in all " (*I Corinthians* 15.28). And on the same lines is that great cry of triumph in *I Corinthians* 3.22, 23 : " All (things) are yours; and ye are Christ's; and Christ is God's."

No one ever had a higher conception of Jesus Christ than Paul had, and yet it is still true to say that for Paul nothing was ever allowed to detract from the lonely supremacy of God. The work of the Son is ever done in obedience to the Father. Behind every event, action and word in the life of Jesus stands God.

It is here we come to one of the most difficult doctrines in all theology, the pre-existence of the Son. We usually consider that doctrine a characteristic of the thought of John. But it is in Paul too. We get a glimpse of that belief in the strange old story which Paul uses in *I Corinthians* 10.4. The Rabbis had a legend that the rock from which the Israelites drank in the desert followed them for ever after in their wanderings, and was to them a continual source of refreshment. Paul refers to that legend and uses it; and then he adds the comment : " That rock was Christ." Whatever else he means, he means that the spiritual refreshing power of the Son goes back to the days of Israel in the desert.

In *Ephesians* 3.11 he speaks of " the eternal purpose which God purposed in Jesus Christ." That is to say, before time and the world began, the work of Christ was in the mind, the plan, the purpose of God. In *Colossians* 1.15 Paul speaks of Jesus Christ as the image of the invisible God, and the first-born of every creature. Certainly in Paul's mind was this conception which we call the pre-existence of the Son.

How can we explain that doctrine to ourselves in such a way that it will really mean something? No one can fully explain it or understand it, but there are two ways in which we can think of it.

First, there is a very simple way. At its simplest this doctrine means that God was always like Jesus. It means that God was not once stern and hard and austere and severe, a God of judgment and of wrath, and then that he suddenly became gentle and gracious and loving towards men. It means that before time began God was like Jesus. It means that in Jesus we see God as God always was, and is, and ever shall be.

Second, there is a more complicated way in which we can try to explain this. God is Father, Son and Holy Spirit. That is the doctrine of the Trinity. Now we connect God the Father with the life-giving work of creation; we connect God the Son with the saving work of redemption; we connect God the Spirit with the illuminating work of revelation. But we must strenuously avoid one mistake. We are very apt to think of this as a kind of series in time. We are apt to think of God first as Creator, then second and afterwards as Redeemer, then still later, as Enlightener and Illuminer. We are apt to think of God creating the world, and then, when the world went wrong, setting out to redeem the world, and then still later, when Jesus had left the earth sending the illumination of the Holy Spirit. But what the doctrine of the Trinity says is that God is always, from before time, through time, and when time shall end, Creator, Redeemer, Sustainer and Enlightener. Through all eternity God creates and is still creating; through all eternity God redeems and is redeeming; through all eternity God sustains and enlightens and is still sustaining and enlightening.

To speak of the pre-existence of the Son is to say that God did not begin to redeem men when Jesus Christ came into this world, but that throughout all ages the redeeming power and the sacrificial work of God had been at work. To speak of the pre-existence of the Son means that the love which was demonstrated on Calvary is an eternal movement of the heart of God to men.

VII

THE INCARNATION

The central fact of Christianity is that in Jesus Christ God came into this world, that in Jesus Christ God took the life of man upon himself. This is the doctrine we call the Incarnation, for the word *Incarnation* literally means *the becoming flesh*. How that could happen men are still trying to explain, and throughout the ages, they have worked out their theories. The method we may never know; the fact we most certainly and blessedly do know. Paul saw the Incarnation from two sides.

Paul saw the Incarnation from the side of God, the Father. To Paul the Incarnation was in the most literal sense an act of God. God sent his Son in flesh like the flesh of any man (*Romans* 8.3). It is the love of God which is in Jesus Christ our Lord (*Romans* 8.39). It was God who was in Christ reconciling the world unto himself (*II Corinthians* 5.19). That gift is an unspeakable gift (*II Corinthians* 9.15). Before such an act of love, in face of such a splendour of generosity, there is nothing left for man but silent and grateful adoration. The Incarnation in its essence is an act of God on behalf of man.

Paul saw the Incarnation from the side of Jesus Christ the Son. Here Paul saw the Incarnation in a way that is uniquely his own. He did not think of the sacrifice of Christ as beginning upon earth. He did not think of the sacrifice of Christ in terms only of the terrible things which happened to him in this world, and which ended in the breaking of his heart by men's disloyalty, and the breaking of his body on the Cross. Paul thought of the sacrifice of Christ as beginning in eternity. Paul was haunted by the thought of what Jesus Christ gave up in order to become man. He could never forget how Jesus Christ laid aside his glory for the humiliation of manhood. With a wonder

which throbs through even the written word, he says:
" Though he was rich, yet for your sakes he became poor "
(*II Corinthians* 8.9). To Paul the sacrifice of Jesus Christ
was a sacrifice which began before time and the world; it
was something which had its beginning in eternity.

The theologians call this the kenotic theory of the Incarnation. The Greek verb *kenoun* means *to empty*; and the
noun *kenōsis* means *an emptying*. And the idea is that,
Jesus Christ, the Son of God, deliberately and sacrificially
emptied himself of his divine glory in order to become man.

The thought of Paul finds its fullest expression in *Philippians* 2.5-11. There Paul speaks of Christ Jesus who had
equality with God as a right, and not a thing to be snatched
at; but he gave it up and did not hug it to himself, and he
became a man. Then Paul goes on to heap up the things
which show the extent of this self-emptying. If God had
come into this world, he might have been expected to come
as a great king in power and might and glory, and with all
the magnificence that the world could give. But Jesus
became of no reputation; he became, not a king, but a
servant. He came, not to order, but to obey. He became
obedient unto death; and that death was not only a natural
death, it was the death of the Cross. As every piece in the
pattern of this passage falls into place, it stresses the extent
and the completeness of the self-emptying of God which the
Incarnation involves.

The strange thing about this *kenōsis* theory is that it
baffles the mind and yet moves the heart. It baffles the
mind to see how God could abandon his essential attributes
and still remain God. God is omniscient, and yet it is clear
that in his earthly life there were things which Jesus did not
know. He often asked questions, and when he did so we
dare not think that he was simply play-acting. He said
himself that not even he knew the day and the hour when
the Son of Man would come in his glory (*Mark* 13.32).

God is omnipotent; and yet it is clear that there were
things which Jesus in his earthly life could not do. Even
that gospel which contains the highest view of Jesus, still
shows us Jesus tired and weary and physically exhausted

with the journey (*John* 4.6). Mark tells us how, when they crossed the lake in the fishing boat, Jesus was asleep on a pillow in the stern of the boat (*Mark* 4.38), and the eternal God neither slumbers nor sleeps.

God is omnipresent; and yet it is clear that during his earthly life Jesus was subject to the laws of space and time, and like any other man could only be in one place at one time.

When we try to grapple with this idea of the self-emptying of God in the Incarnation, the mind cannot grasp it. We may make it a little easier for our minds to think of, if we say that in the Incarnation God emptied himself of his purely metaphysical attributes, such as omniscience, omnipotence and omnipresence; but not of his moral attributes, his goodness, his justice and, above all, his love.

The self-emptying of God in the Incarnation is the supreme demonstration of his love, for it was of his love that he wished to tell men, and it was about his love that men above all needed to know.

It may be that this Pauline idea of the divine *kenōsis*, the self-emptying of God is something which the mind cannot grasp and cannot explain; but for the heart it does set out, as no other doctrine does, the unimaginable sacrifice of love which God made in becoming man at all. It sets out what God had to give up in order to come into this world for us men and for our salvation.

More than once Paul stresses the reality of the Incarnation. We have already seen how in *Philippians* 2.5-11 Paul stresses the completeness of the Incarnation. In *Romans* 1.3 he speaks of Jesus being made of the seed of David according to the flesh. The actual physical descent of Jesus is laid down at the very beginning of the letter. In *Romans* 8.3 he speaks of God sending his Son in the likeness of, in the guise of, as Moffatt puts it, sinful flesh. We find this same insistence on the reality of the Incarnation in John's First Letter. John writes: " Every spirit that confesseth that Jesus Christ is come in the flesh is of God : and every spirit that confesseth not that Jesus Christ is come in the flesh is not of God " (*I John* 4.2, 3).

Both Paul and John were directing their teaching against a heresy which is known as Docetism. We have seen how the Gnostics believed that matter was essentially flawed and essentially evil. If that be so, then quite obviously the body must be essentially an evil thing. These Gnostics taught that Jesus had not a real body at all; that He was a kind of ghost or phantom with a body which was made of spirit and not of flesh. *Dokein* means *to seem*; and these Gnostics taught that Jesus seemed to be a man, had the appearance of being a man, but in reality had no human body at all.

The Gnostics produced many books which purported to be lives of Jesus. One of them is called The Acts of John and it was written about A.D. 150. In it John is represented as saying about Jesus : " Sometimes when I would lay hold on him, I met with a material and solid body, and at other times again, when I felt him, the substance was immaterial and as if it existed not at all . . . And often-times when I walked with him, I desired to see the print of his foot, whether it appeared on the earth; and I never saw it."

To these Gnostics Jesus was a phantom figure who looked like a man but who was not. Paul would have none of that; he insisted that Jesus was really and truly man. As we shall see, in Paul's thought it was completely essential that Jesus must be completely man, if ever he was to redeem man. And Paul would have nothing to do with any of these theories which tried to honour the divinity of Jesus by destroying his humanity.

Paul regarded the Incarnation as an act of the love of God; he regarded the Incarnation as involving the beginning of Jesus Christ's sacrifice in eternity and before time; he regarded the Incarnation as involving the full and complete humanity of the Son of God. For Paul the manhood of Jesus was of supreme importance, because Paul was quite clear that we are saved as much by the life of Jesus as by his death. For Paul the life of Christ is every bit as necessary an element in salvation as the death of Christ. We must look in detail at this idea in Paul, for it is the key to one of the most difficult chapters that Paul ever wrote.

Twice this idea of the efficacy of the life of Jesus in the

work of salvation emerges. It emerges briefly in *I Corin-thians* 15.21, 22 : "Since by man came death, by man came also the resurrection from the dead; for as in Adam all die, even so in Christ shall all be made alive." But this idea emerges most fully in *Romans* 5.12-21. The basic idea of that passage is stated in verse 19 : "As by one man's dis-obedience many were made sinners, so by the obedience of one shall many be made righteous."

The argument of this passage is that all men sinned in Adam. We must note carefully that Paul is not saying that all men sinned in the same way as Adam sinned. He is not saying that from Adam men inherited the tendency to sin. He is saying that all mankind literally and actually sinned in Adam. The fact that Adam sinned constituted all men sinners.

To a twentieth-century western mind that is a very dif-ficult, if not an impossible idea. We find it very difficult to understand how all men, how we, sinned in Adam. At the back of it there is the Jewish idea of solidarity. This is an idea which is characteristic of the primitive thinking of most nations. The Jew never thought of himself as an individual; he always thought of himself as the member of a family, a clan, or a nation. Apart from that family, clan, or nation he had no separate existence. He existed not as an indi-vidual, but as a unit in a society. To this day it is said that an Australian aborigine, on being asked his name, will give, not his own name, but the name of his tribe. He thinks of himself first and foremost as a member of a tribe. This is most clearly seen in action in the blood feud. Sup-pose a man of one tribe is injured or killed by a man of another tribe. Then it becomes the duty of the whole tribe of the injured man to take vengeance on the whole tribe of the injurer. The whole tribe is thought of as involved in the injury : and the whole tribe is thought of as inflicting the injury. The matter is not a matter of individuals at all; it is a matter of tribes; that is solidarity in action.

We have a vivid example of this principle in action in the Old Testament in *Joshua* 7. At the conquest of Jericho, Achan had kept to himself certain of the spoils in direct disobedience to the commandment of God that all the spoils should be destroyed; and at first no one knew of Achan's secret disobedience. After the fall of Jericho the Israelites moved on to take Ai, which should have fallen without any trouble at all. It did not; the siege of Ai produced disaster. Why? Because Achan had sinned by disobedience. The sin of Achan had constituted the whole nation one corporate sinner and on the nation God was sending his punishment. Achan was not an individual; he had no separate existence apart from the nation; he was part of the nation; and in his sin the whole nation had sinned, and for his sin the whole nation was being punished. What the individual did, the nation did. Further, when it was discovered that it was Achan who had sinned, not only was Achan executed, but his whole family was also executed with him, for they were involved in his sin. Here then is solidarity.

Paul begins with the idea that quite literally all men sinned in Adam; all men were involved in Adam's sin; because Adam became a sinner all the descendants of Adam were constituted sinners.

But it might well be said to Paul : "How can you prove that? That is an extraordinary statement to make. Can you advance any proof that in fact all men did sin in Adam?" It is that proof which Paul seeks to advance in *Romans* 5. In Paul's argument there are certain basic steps.

1. Basic to Paul's argument is the insistence that death is the consequence of sin. Death came by sin (*Romans* 5.12). Had there been no sin, there would have been no death. Death is the result of sin.

2. Adam broke a positive commandment of God, the commandment not to eat of the fruit of the forbidden tree. Thereby Adam sinned; and thereby Adam became liable to death (*Romans* 5.12).

3. But how can Paul prove that in that particular sin of Adam all sinned? The Law did not come into the world until the time of Moses. Now, if there is no Law, there can be no sin, for sin is a breach of the Law. Therefore before Moses there could be no such thing as sin. Between Adam

and Moses the Law did not exist; therefore sin did not exist. *And yet men died.* That is the argument of *Romans* 5.13, 14.

4. Why then should men die, if there was no Law, and therefore no sin? The answer is that they died because they had sinned in Adam; they were involved in Adam's sin; by one man's offence death reigned by one (*Romans* 5.17).

It is Paul's argument that the fact that men continued to die before the beginning of the Law, and therefore before there could be such a thing as sin, is the proof of the fact that they had sinned in Adam. By the sin of Adam all men were constituted sinners.

And now we come to the other side of the argument. Into this world came Christ. He brought to God the perfect righteousness and the perfect obedience (*Romans* 5.18, 19). And just as all men were involved in Adam's sin, so all men were involved in Jesus Christ's perfect obedience, and perfect goodness, and perfect holiness. By that perfect obedience of Jesus Christ, the evil and unending chain of sin and death was broken; the deadly series was interrupted; the new holiness entered in. And just as men had been constituted sinners by Adam's sin, they were constituted righteous by Jesus Christ's obedience. In view of the conception of solidarity mankind was involved in the sin of Adam; and in view of the conception of solidarity mankind is involved in the holiness of Christ. The sin of Adam made all men sinners; the obedience of Christ made all men righteous.

Now it is completely clear that the argument of Paul rests on the fact that Jesus Christ was fully man. The whole argument collapses unless Jesus is as human as Adam was human. For the arguments to be valid the Incarnation must be absolutely real. Mankind must be as fully identified with Christ as once it was with Adam.

To our modern minds all this is a strange argument. We find it hard to grasp, and, if we are honest, many of us will have to say that we do not find it very convincing. But in this argument there is one great flaw and there is one great truth.

The flaw lies in this. Suppose we take the Adam story

quite literally. Suppose we assume that it is literally true that Adam was the first man, and that we are all his descendants. Then the conclusion is that our connection with Adam is a physical connection. It is something which we can neither choose nor reject. We have no choice whatever in the matter. It is simply an inevitable matter of physical descent. But on the other hand, our connection with Jesus Christ is a spiritual connection. It is by no means an inevitable relationship; it is something which we can either accept or reject. The connection is quite different. No man can reasonably be condemned because he is physically connected with his ancestors; but any man must bear the responsibility for accepting or refusing his connection with Jesus Christ. That is the flaw in Paul's argument.

But there is also in Paul's argument an eternal truth. The truth is this. Man was involved in a situation from which he could not free himself; he was dominated by sin; he was helplessly in the grip of sin. Into this situation came Christ, with a power which could break into this hopeless situation and introduce a new element of release. What is true is that man was hopelessly and helplessly involved in sin, and that Christ liberated him from that tragic and impotent situation. Through Jesus Christ, man the sinner becomes potentially man the righteous. As Paul would have said, the sin of Adam made men sinners; the holiness of Christ can make men holy.

VIII

THE WORK OF CHRIST

As we study the writings of Paul we come upon picture after picture of what Jesus Christ has done for man.

In the very forefront of Paul's thought was the fact that Jesus Christ brought to men a knowledge of God which without him they could never have possessed or entered into. Jesus himself said : " He that hath seen me hath seen the Father " (*John* 14.9), and that was an essential and primary part of the belief of Paul. To put it at its simplest, Paul believed with all his heart that Jesus has shown us what God is like. God commanded the light to shine out of the darkness " to give the light of knowledge of the glory of God in the face of Jesus Christ " (*II Corinthians* 4.6). Jesus is the revelation of the glory of God; he is the incarnate glory; in him men see the glory of God.

It is in the letter to the Colossians that this idea emerges in all its splendour. That letter was written to combat a heresy which held that Jesus was certainly great, but that he was only one stage on the way to the knowledge of God. Paul will have none of that. For him there was nothing partial about Jesus Christ. Jesus was the full revelation of God. " It pleased the Father," he writes, " that in him should all fulness dwell " (*Colossians* 1.19). He speaks of Christ " in whom are hid all the treasures of wisdom and knowledge " (*Colossians* 2.3). And then he goes on to make the statement beyond which no statement about Jesus Christ can go : " In him dwelleth all the fulness of the Godhead bodily " (*Colossians* 2.9).

It is not so much that Jesus came to bring the full revelation of God. It is not that he came to write a book, or to give a course of sermons or lectures on what God is like. Rather he came to *be* the full revelation of God. It is not as if Paul said : " Listen to Jesus Christ, and you will learn

55

what God is like." It is as if he said : " Look at Jesus Christ
and you will see what God is." That seeking for sinners,
that care for sufferers, that feeding of the hungry, that
comforting of the sorrowing, that sacrificial love for men is
a demonstration in time of the eternal attitude of God to
men.

But it would not be enough simply to show men what
God was like. That in itself might even be a torturing and
haunting thing. It might be like allowing a man a glimpse
of some warmth and splendour into which he himself could
never enter. It might simply be to tantalise a man with a
vision of beauty which could never be anything other than
something seen at a great distance. As Paul saw it, Jesus
Christ came to open the way to God for men, to give men
access to God.

Paul speaks of the access we have to grace through Jesus
Christ. He speaks of those who were far off being brought
near (*Ephesians* 2.13). He says that through him we have
access unto the Father (*Ephesians* 2.18; 3.12). The word
which Paul uses for *access* is of supreme interest. It is the
noun *prosagōgē* which is connected with the verb *prosagein*.
In the Greek version of the Old Testament, *prosagein* is the
word which is used of bringing men to God that they may
be ordained as priests for his service (*Exodus* 29.4).

Even the heathen world would see the greatness of the
meaning of this word. The main form of Greek religion in
the time of Paul was the Mystery Religions. They were like
passion plays; and the worshipper was only allowed to
attend them after a long course of instruction and training
and discipline had prepared him to become an initiate.
When he was so prepared, it was the duty of an official
called a *mustagōgos* to bring him in, and the word for
bringing in such an initiate is *prosagein*.

It is perhaps even more suggestive that this word had a
use which was connected specially with the court of kings.
Prosagein is the regular word for introducing a person into
the presence of a king. Xenophon tells for instance how
Astyages the king had a trusted official called Sacas, who
was his cup-bearer, and who had the responsibility of intro-

ducing (*prosagein*) to the king those whom he thought to have a right to that privilege, and of keeping out those whom he did not think fit for it. There was in fact at the Persian court a court official whose title in Greek was *prosagōgeus*, the introducer, the person who was responsible for ushering others into the presence of the king. So then, to Paul, Jesus was the person who was able and willing to introduce men into the presence of God.

Behind that thought of Jesus Christ as the introducer into the presence of God there were in Paul's mind two thoughts. The first is that men by their sin had erected a barrier between themselves and God, and Jesus removed that barrier and opened the way. We must leave the fuller discussion of that until later. But Paul would have agreed with all his heart that the love of Christ had broken every barrier down.

But in Paul's mind there was certainly another idea. We have already said that Jesus Christ came into this world to show men what God is. The fact is that until Jesus came into the world men had a wrong idea of God. They thought of God as the task-master, the lawgiver, the judge. They thought of God as that awful purity before whom every man is in default, and from whom every man can expect nothing but condemnation. They thought of God as that inexorable justice, which was bound to utter sentence of condemnation. They thought of God as the implacable hunter bent on the destruction of the sinner. Clearly men who held that idea would have but one idea—not to approach God, but to flee from his presence and to escape from his wrath, an obviously impossible task.

But the coming of Jesus Christ showed God in an entirely new light. His life of service and his death of love gave men a completely new idea of God. It showed God to men as the lover of the souls of men. It showed God as seeking love. It showed God as the God whose one desire is to forgive and to gather men to himself in fatherly love. It banished the fear of approaching God from the hearts of men. It opened a way to God for men whose one desire and instinct had been to flee from God. Apart from Jesus

Christ men never could have known the love of God. And that new revelation, and that new discovery opened a door of access to God, for it made men able to cast themselves on the love of God instead of fleeing for ever from the wrath of God.

In the course of his writings Paul uses six great metaphors to describe the work of Jesus Christ. He takes six great pictures from ordinary life everyday to show to men what Jesus Christ has done. These pictures would be very vivid to those who heard them for the first time, for they came from spheres which they all knew and understood; and they are still capable of becoming real for us today.

The first great metaphor is *the metaphor from the law courts,* the metaphor of *justification.* Christianity, like Judaism before it, is essentially an ethical religion. That is to say, Christianity insists that a man should live a certain kind of life and be a certain kind of person. It is God's will and God's commandment that he should do and be so. An ethical religion must always have sanctions. That is to say, there must be a difference between what happens in eternity to the man who has fulfilled the ethical demand of his religion and the man who has not. To put that in another way, it means that there must be judgment. Some day a man must stand his trial before God; he must appear before God's judgment seat; he must give account for the things done in his body (*Romans* 14.10, 12). If that be so, every man must stand in default, for no human being can possibly fulfil the demands of the perfection of God.

It is just here that justification comes in. Justification pictures a man on trial before God. Paul says: "Being justified by faith, we have peace with God through our Lord Jesus Christ" (*Romans* 5.1). He says that it is true that we have all sinned, but we are justified freely through his grace (*Romans* 3.24). We are justified by faith (*Romans* 3.28). God, says Paul in a magnificent phrase, justifies the ungodly (*Romans* 4.5).

In the New Testament, especially in Paul, the verb *to justify,* when it is used of God, has a very different sense from that which it has in English. In English to justify a person means to produce reasons why he was right, to bring forward arguments which prove, or attempt to prove, that he was perfectly correct, to act as he did. If I justify myself, using the word in its English sense, it means that I seek to produce reasons in defence of any action that I have taken. But that is not at all what the word means in the New Testament. In Greek the word for *to justify* is *dikaioun*. Greek verbs which end in *-oun* do not mean to make a person something; they mean to treat, to reckon, to account a man as being something. And when Paul speaks of God justifying the sinner, he means that God, instead of punishing the sinner, instead of issuing penalty like a righteous but merciless judge, treats the sinner as if he had been a good man.

This is exactly what shocked the Jews to the very core of their being. For any judge to treat a bad man as if he was a good man was to the Jew the acme of injustice and wickedness. The Old Testament has it : " He that justifieth the wicked is an abomination to the Lord (*Proverbs* 17.15). God says : " I will not justify the wicked " (*Exodus* 23.7). In face of that Paul comes with the audacious and the tremendous paradox that God is characteristically the God who justifies the ungodly (*Romans* 4.5).

The whole essence of the gospel which Paul came to preach is that God, in this astounding mercy, treats the sinner as if he had been a good man. Instead of smashing the sinner, he welcomes him with open arms. Instead of outpouring the mighty vials of his outraged holiness, he pours out the cleansing waters of his sacrificial love.

When the American Civil War was in progress, and when the South had rebelled against the North on the question of slavery, someone once asked Lincoln : " When this war is over, and when the South has been subdued and conquered, and has come back into the Union, how are you going to treat these rebellious southerners, what are you going to do to them?" Back came Lincoln's answer : " I am going to treat them as if they had never been away." That is precisely what Paul means by justification; he means that in that astonishing love, God treats men as if they had never been away.

We so often think of justification as a theological and even a remote, conception; but the perfect picture of justification lies in the Parable of the Prodigal Son. The son has planned to come back with his confession of sin against heaven and his father, and with his request to be made a hired servant. He is never allowed to make that request (*Luke* 15.18, 19, 21). His father welcomes him back, not to the status of servant, but to the status of son, as if he had never been away.

A Sunday school teacher was once telling the story of the Prodigal Son to a class in a slum mission in Scotland. She told the story of the son's rebellion, of his terrible fate in the far country, of his resolution to come home. And she went on, " What do you think his father would do to him when he got home?" From that class of slum children, who knew life at its toughest, back came the immediate answer : "Bash him!" That is the natural answer; that is what anyone would expect; but that is the wrong answer, for the glory of God is that God justifies the ungodly. He treats the bad man as if he had been good.

Of course there is more to it than that; the process does not stop there; justification has to be followed by *sanctification*. The sinner who has been so freely received back has to go on to clothe himself with the lost holiness. But the first step in the process of salvation is the simple, yet utterly tremendous, fact that God justifies the ungodly, treats the rebellious as if he had never rebelled.

But, we must go on to ask, why justification *by faith*? What is the meaning of the words *by faith*? The answer to that lies in another question : How can we believe that God is like that? All our instincts would make us think of God as the judge, God dealing out strict and impartial justice, and of ourselves standing at the judgment seat of God as criminals condemned, and justly, for their misdeeds. How can we know that God is not like that, that in fact his one desire is to welcome the sinner home? We can only know that because Jesus told us so. We have to put our whole faith in the assumption that Jesus was right when he told us that God is like that. Faith is staking everything on the fact that God is like Jesus, that Jesus was right when he told of the God who welcomes sinners home. Faith is accepting Jesus at his word when he brings to men the offer of God.

That then is the first great metaphor which Paul uses to describe the work of Christ. It is the message that the just shall live by faith (*Galatians* 3.11); that by works of the law shall no flesh be justified (*Galatians* 2.16). It is the message that we receive a right relationship with God, not through our own efforts to achieve the hopeless task of pleasing God, but by accepting just as we are, the offer of his love. When Paul speaks of the man who is just, he means the man who is in a right relationship with God. That relationship cannot be won; it must be accepted in the certainty that God treats the bad man as if he had never been away.

Here is the metaphor from the law courts. It shows us man standing before God with the right to expect nothing but utter condemnation; and suddenly discovering through the message of Jesus Christ that God is not threatening him with austere justice but is offering him amazing love.

The highest thought of the Jewish Rabbis had faint glimpses of this. One Rabbi heard God say : "Return as far as you can, and I will come to you the rest of the way." God is always ready to meet the sinner more than half-way. Another Rabbi said : "Beloved is repentance before God, for he cancels his own words for its sake."

Such is the love of God that he cancels the demands of his own justice upon men. That is what justification means. It means that the sinner is not a condemned criminal; he is a lost son, whom God will treat as if he had never been away, if he will only turn and come home.

The second of the great metaphors which Paul uses to describe the work of Christ is the *metaphor from friendship*. This picture is contained in the word *reconciliation*. The Greek verb for *to reconcile* is *katallassein*. It is not that Paul uses this metaphor very often, but, when he does use it, it is at the very heart of his gospel.

He speaks about us being enemies to God, and being reconciled by the death of his Son (*Romans* 5.10). In *II Corinthians* 5.18, 20, there are three occurrences of this word and of this idea. God has reconciled us to himself by Jesus Christ. God was in Christ reconciling the world unto himself. And Paul's appeal is : " Be ye reconciled to God." In *Ephesians* Paul speaks of how God reconciled Jew and Gentile to each other, and both to God (*Ephesians* 2.16). In *Colossians* he speaks of it being God's aim to reconcile all things unto himself by Jesus Christ (*Colossians* 1.20). " You," he says, " who were sometime alienated and enemies in your mind by wicked works, yet now hath he reconciled " (*Colossians* 1.21).

The key to this idea is the restoration of a lost relationship. Because of man's sin and disobedience and rebelliousness the relationship which exists between man and God is a compound of estrangement, enmity and fear; but because of what Jesus Christ has done that grim relationship is replaced by a relationship of trusting love. It is the removal of the barriers, the substitution of a relationship of love for a relationship of fear, a relationship of intimacy for a relationship of distance.

One thing has to be noted, Paul never speaks of God being reconciled to men, but always of men being reconciled to God. The breach was not on God's side, but on man's side. It is as if God sent Jesus Christ into this world to live, to suffer and to die, as if to say : " I love you like that. Surely you cannot shut your heart to me and resist me any more."

This is the simplest of all the pictures. Reconciliation means bringing together again two people who have become estranged; and Jesus Christ brought man and God together again.

The third of Paul's metaphors is the *metaphor from slavery*. The ancient world was built on slavery. It may be that most of the Church's members were slaves or had been slaves, and this picture would be very real to them. It is the picture in the words *redemption*, and *purchase at a price*.

This picture has two backgrounds which share equally in giving it its meaning.

It has a Hebrew background. In the Old Testament this idea of redemption (*lutrōsis*) is intimately bound up with the thought of the emancipation of the people from Egypt. To the Jews that liberation from their slavery in Egypt was the supreme event in their history, and the supreme intervention of God. "I will redeem you," said God, "with a stretched out arm" (*Exodus* 6.6). "Thou in thy mercy hast led forth thy people whom thou hast redeemed" (*Exodus* 15.13). "The Lord hath redeemed you out of the house of bondmen" (*Deuteronomy* 7.8). Again and again the text occurs in one form or another: "Thou shalt remember that thou wast a bondman in the land of Egypt and the Lord thy God redeemed thee" (*Deuteronomy* 15.15; 16.12).

Through this picture there throbs the joy of the slave set free. The Jews never forgot how God had interposed to liberate them from slavery in Egypt. This is the metaphor of liberty regained by the intervention of God.

But this picture has also a Greek background. It was possible in Greece for a slave with a great effort to purchase his own freedom. The method by which he did so was rather a lovely thing. The slave would decide to make the great effort. In the little spare time he had he would take any job that he could get in order to earn a few coppers. By the laws of slavery he could not keep even all the little that he did earn. His master was entitled to claim a percentage of it. The little he did keep the slave deposited in the temple of some god. The years passed by and the day came when the slave had accumulated enough to pay for the purchase price of his freedom. The slave then took his master to the temple, and the priest paid over the money to the master; the result was that the slave became the property of the god, and therefore free from all men.

It is that picture which is in Paul's mind when he says: "Ye are bought with a price" (*I Corinthians* 6.20). "Ye are bought with a price; be not ye the servants of men" (*I Corinthians* 7.23). The slave was free of all men because he had become the possession of the god who, it was held, had paid his price.

There is no doubt that that picture of the way in which a slave obtained his liberty by becoming the possession of a god was in Paul's mind; but it is clear that that metaphor is not to be overpressed. In that kind of liberation and emancipation the slave saved until he had amassed his own purchase price; in a sense he was his own liberator. Paul would not for a moment have held that we could pay our own purchase price. This is a good example of a Pauline metaphor which must be taken in its general idea, and not pressed overmuch in detail.

Whatever its background this picture of freedom, of emancipation, of liberty regained is much in Paul's mind. He writes to the Romans of the Christian being justified freely by God's grace, through the redemption that is through Jesus Christ (*Romans* 3.24). To the Corinthians he writes that Jesus is made by God righteousness, and sanctification, and redemption (*I Corinthians* 1.30). To the Ephesians he writes of the Christian having redemption through the blood of Christ, and forgiveness of sins according to the riches of his grace (*Ephesians* 1.7). To the Colossians he speaks of Jesus Christ in whom we have redemption through his blood, even the forgiveness of sins (*Colossians* 1.14).

Here indeed is a metaphor and a picture which speaks to our condition. In so many cases, and so often, life is a slavery, bound in the chains of our own forging. For many of us it is true to say that the only reason why we are not better than we are is that we cannot make ourselves better. There are weaknesses within us that we cannot conquer. There are habits that we cannot break. There is a past which has us in its shackles. There are ingrained things which we cannot escape. We have incurred a condemnation from which there can be no acquittal that we could ever win.

Jesus Christ liberates us from ourselves. Eric Linklater called his autobiography *The Man Upon My Back*. For so many of us our greatest handicap is our own selves; and

Jesus Christ gives us the strength and power to conquer ourselves.

Jesus Christ liberates us from frustration. Another way of putting that is that the tragedy of the human situation is that we know what is right, and we cannot do it. We have seen the dream and we cannot achieve it. We are haunted by the impossibilities of life. Jesus Christ gives us the power which makes the impossible possible.

Jesus Christ liberates us from fear. So many people live in a fear-haunted life; but Jesus offers us his continual presence in which fear must die, for with him we can face and do anything.

Jesus Christ liberates us from sin. Through what he has done the sin of the past is cancelled, and into life there comes a strength in which the temptations of the future can be conquered. Sin's penalty is removed and sin's power is broken by the work of Christ. Redemption is the metaphor of liberation from slavery. Jesus Christ is the great emancipator of all mankind.

There is one picture of the work of Jesus Christ which for Paul was very near the heart of things. It is the idea which the Authorized Version renders by the word *propitiation*. The central passage is in *Romans* 3.25 where Paul speaks of Jesus, "whom God sent forth as a propitiation through faith in his blood". This is an idea which is at the very heart of Jewish religion and at the very centre of the experience of Paul. The word for *propitiation* is *hilastērion*, the precise meaning of which we shall have to go on to discuss. But first of all let us try to penetrate to the idea which lies behind it.

The word *hilastērion* is connected with the verb *hilaskesthai*, which in turn is connected with the adjective *hileōs*. We shall best get at its meaning if we start from the adjective. *Hileōs*, the adjective, means *gracious*, *well disposed to*. So, then, the verb *hilaskesthai* means *to make*, or *to become*, *gracious to*. It means to make expiation for sin, and when it is used of God it means quite simply to forgive.

The basic idea is the turning of wrath into graciousness,

the change from being hostile into being well-disposed to a
person.

Behind this word there lies all the meaning of the whole
institution of sacrifice. The basic idea of sacrifice is this—
there are certain things that a man must not do, for if he
does them he invades the prerogatives of God; he trans-
gresses the law of God; he rebels against God. Clearly, if a
man is guilty of any such action, the relationship which
should exist between him and God is broken and interrupted. The problem then is, how can that relationship be
restored? That is where sacrifice comes in. Sacrifice is that
which restores the lost and broken relationship between man
and God. It is to be clearly remembered that in any real
religion, and certainly in Jewish religion, it was not the
sacrifice itself which restored the relationship; it was the
penitence of which the sacrifice was a sign, a symbol, a
guarantee and a proof.

The idea is quite simple. A man sins; a man realises
what he has done; a man repents. But how can he guarantee and prove that that penitence is real and genuine? He
can only do so by offering to God something precious in
order to show how really and truly sorry he is. That is the
true idea of sacrifice. The important thing is not the sacrifice itself; the important thing is the real penitence and
sorrow of which the actual sacrifice is only the outward
expression.

So, then, Paul says that Jesus is our *hilastērion*. What is
the meaning of that word? If the word be taken as a noun,
there are two suggestions. (*a*) It is suggested that *hilastērion*
means *a sacrifice to expiate sin*. This would mean that Jesus
is the sacrifice who expiates the sin of man. Nowhere in all
Greek literature does *hilastērion* mean a sacrifice, nor is it
possible that the word can mean sacrifice. That is a meaning of the word which we shall have to discard.

(*b*) There is one thing which *hilastērion* can mean, if it is
a noun, and which, in fact, it does regularly mean both in
the Old and in the New Testament. All Greek nouns which
end in *-ērion* mean *the place where something is done*.
Dikastērion means the place where *dikē*, justice is done

and therefore a law court. *Thusiastērion* means the place where *thusia*, sacrifice is done, and therefore the altar. Therefore *hilastērion* can certainly mean the place where *hilasmos*, expiation, is done and made. Because of that, both in the Old and New Testament, *hilastērion* has a regular and a technical meaning. It always means the lid of gold above the ark which was known as *the mercy-seat*. In *Exodus* 25.17 it is laid down of the furnishings of the tabernacle: "Thou shalt make a mercy-seat (*hilastērion*) of pure gold." In only one other place in the New Testament is the word used, in *Hebrews* 9.5, and there the writer speaks of the cherubim who overshadow the mercy-seat. The word is used in that sense more than twenty times in the Greek Old Testament.

Now there were two special ideas attaching to the mercy-seat. The mercy-seat as we have seen was the golden lid of the ark which rested in the Holy of Holies. Into the Holy of Holies only the High Priest might enter, and there the High Priest, representing the people, held communion with God. It was God's promise : " I will meet with thee, and I will commune with thee from above the mercy seat " (*Exodus* 25.22). God promised : " I will appear in the cloud above the mercy seat " (*Leviticus* 16.2). The mercy-seat was above all the place where God and his people met.

But there was another ceremony connected with the mercy-seat. It was on the Day of Atonement that sacrifices were made which atoned for all the sins, known and unknown, of the people. And it was on the mercy-seat that the blood of the sacrifices was sprinkled (*Leviticus* 16.14, 15). The result of that sacrifice and that sprinkling of blood was that the people would be cleansed from all their sins (*Leviticus* 16.30). Therefore the mercy-seat was the place where the blood which atoned for sin was shed.

If then we take *hilastērion* to mean the mercy-seat, and, if we call Jesus our *hilastērion* in that sense, it will mean, so to speak, that Jesus is the place where man and God meet, and that specially he is the place where man's sin meets with the atoning love of God.

That is a tremendous thought. It is the thought that the

death of Jesus Christ, the Cross, is the trysting-place where God's justice and God's mercy meet. It means that on the Cross we see the mercy of God offering the sacrifice for the sin of man which his justice demands. That is one way of looking at what happened on the Cross.

There are in God two essential attributes. The first is his love; that love of God demands and insists that God must forgive. The second is his justice; that justice of God demands and insists that man's sin must be punished. Here is what in all reverence we may call the dilemma of God. God's love necessitates the forgiveness of sin; God's justice necessitates the punishment of sin. What can God do? The answer is that on the Cross, in Jesus Christ, God's love pays the penalty and bears the punishment which God's justice demands. On the Cross, in Jesus Christ, God's love and God's justice meet, in the one possible act which could satisfy both that justice and that love. Here, indeed, is a most moving thought on which the mind can feed and the heart can rest.

(c) But there is another way to take this word *hilastērion*. It is possible, indeed it is more likely, that *hilastērion* is not a noun, but rather an adjective (*hilastērios*), which means *able to make expiation for sin*.

If we take it this way, and it is most likely the right way, in *Romans* 3.25 what Paul is saying is that God set forth Jesus for all men to see, as the only person in all the universe who can bring man back to God, who can restore the lost relationship and who can make expiation for sin. Cranmer translated *hilastērion* as the *obtainer of mercy*; the Geneva Version translated it as the *pacification*. Jesus is the one person able by his life and his death to bring man and God together again.

We are not bound to interpret this great fact in any one way. We may interpret it by saying that Jesus Christ paid the penalty which man's sins had made necessary. We may interpret it by saying that the infinite and tremendous demonstration of the love of God broke men's hearts and destroyed the last barrier. It does not matter how we interpret it, we are back at the truth which is for ever at the centre of the New Testament. It cost the life and death of Christ, it cost the Cross, to restore the lost relationship between God and man.

It was out of the experience of Paul that this idea was born. Think of Paul's background. He was a Jew, and as a Jew he had an intense awareness of the sheer holiness of God. The sense of the holiness of God tortured him with the sense of his own unworthiness, and of the barrier which his sin had erected between himself and God. The religion of his country and his nation believed that sacrifice could remove that barrier. Paul knew that it could not, for he had tried it and it had failed. Then, sudden on a moment, he was confronted with Christ, and the barriers were down, and Paul was at home with God at last. The enmity was gone; the estrangement was destroyed; God was his friend.

Paul, more than once, uses a picture taken from family life to express what God in Jesus Christ did for men. It is the picture of *adoption (huiothesia)*. In *Romans* 8.15 Paul says that the Christian has received the spirit of adoption which enables us to call God Father, and to approach God as such. In *Romans* 8.23 he describes the Christian and all creation as waiting eagerly for the adoption. In *Romans* 9.4 he speaks of the people of Israel as the adopted people of God. In *Galatians* 4.5 he says that God sent his Son to redeem those who were under the law, that they might receive adoption as sons. In *Ephesians* 1.5 he says that it was God's eternal purpose that the Christians should be adopted as children through Jesus Christ.

It is clear that this is an idea which was much in the mind of Paul, and that it was a picture which for him did represent what had happened to the Christian through the work of Jesus Christ.

The idea of adoption would paint an even more vivid picture to the people of the ancient world than it does to us today. Adoption was common in the ancient world. It was carried out for three main reasons—to ensure the continuation of the family and of the family name, to ensure that there was someone to whom the family estates might be passed down, and to ensure that the worship of the family and ancestral gods might go on uninterrupted.

The different sections of the ancient world had their different methods of adoption. Amongst the Jews adoption was not common, and there were no special legal ceremonies connected with it.

Amongst the Greeks the practice of adoption was much commoner and the process was more elaborate. Adoption could only be carried out by persons capable of making a will, that is by men; both parties must be of sound mind; there must be no undue influence; before a man could adopt a son, he must have no legitimate son; that is, he could not adopt a son over the head of an already existing legitimate son. The party to be adopted must be a Greek citizen; if he was of age, his own consent was necessary; if he was a minor, his guardian's consent was necessary; neither the adopter nor the adopted must be guilty of anything which affected his citizenship or his legal status. For instance, a person who for any reason was disfranchised could neither adopt nor be adopted.

The method of adoption was simplicity itself. The Greeks were divided into *phratriai,* which were practically clans, and into *demes* for administrative purposes. And the ceremony of adoption was simply a religious and civil ceremony of adoption into the new clan and enrolment into the new *deme.*

The result of the adoption was that the adopted person lost all rights in his old family and gained all rights in his new family. Even if legitimate children were afterwards born, he inherited fully and without question along with them.

But that which is really in Paul's mind is Roman adoption. There was no more dramatic and far-reaching legal ceremony in any law than Roman adoption. The seriousness and the finality of Roman adoption was due to the fact of the Roman *patria potestas,* the law of the father's power. Under Roman law a Roman father had absolute power over his children. He could sell the child and he could enslave the child. That right even extended to the right of life and death. A Roman father was legally entitled to execute his own child. Under Roman law a son could not himself possess anything, or inherit anything. Anything left to him passed at once into his father's power. Still further, under Roman law so long as his father was alive a son never came of age. He might be a man of very senior years; he might have reached high and noble and honoured office in the state, but so long as his father was alive, he remained entirely in his father's power. Dion Cassius, the Greek historian, describes the situation : " The law of the Romans gives a father absolute authority over his son, and that for the son's whole life. It gives him authority, if he so chooses, to imprison him, to scourge him, to make him work on his estate as a slave in fetters, even to kill him. The right still continues to exist even if the son is old enough to play an active part in political affairs, even if he has been judged worthy to occupy the magistrate's office, and even if he is held in honour by all men."

In Rome there were two main methods of adoption depending on whether the person to be adopted was of age or not. If the person was of age, that is to say, if his father was not alive, the process was called *Adrogatio*. The person to be adopted had to appear before the *Comitia Curiata,* which was the most solemn of all Roman Courts. It was presided over by the *Pontifex Maximus,* the High Priest, and had charge of the ordination of magistrates, the administration of wills, and this kind of adoption.

The adoption was in two stages. First, there came the *Detestatio Sacrorum* : this meant that the man to be adopted had in public to forswear his own family and ancestral gods and to accept as his gods the gods of the family into which he was being adopted. It was a public denial of the old gods, and a public acceptance of the new gods.

Second, there followed a process called *Rogatio* in which a full legal bill embodying the adoption was presented before the *Comitia Curiata* and was voted on in the usual way.

Obviously all this was a most elaborate and impressive ceremony, representing and ratifying a step than which none
could be more serious.

If the person to be adopted was under the legal age the
ceremony was equally dramatic. The child had to pass
from one *patria potestas* to another. It was carried out by a
symbolic sale; the process was called *mancipatio.* Scales
and copper weights were used. Twice the father sold his
son, and twice he bought him back again. Then he sold
him for a third and last time, and the sale was complete.
After that, the three parties, the adopted son, his father, and
the adopter, all appeared before the Roman magistrate
called the *praetor,* and a symbolic lawsuit was carried out,
in which the legal claim for the son to be brought into the
new *patria potestas* was fully argued, and only when that
case was settled was adoption complete.

It can be seen that under Roman law adoption was not
an easy affair; it was regarded as the most decisive of steps;
it could only be taken after the most searching and dramatic
ceremonies had been gone through; and once undertaken
it was finally settled once and for all.

The consequences of Roman adoption were far-reaching.
The adopted son completely lost all rights in his old family
and completely gained all rights in his new family. In the
most literal sense he gained a new father. He became as
fully heir to his new father's estate as any normal son.
According to the law all the debts and obligations of his
former life were cancelled. He was a new person entering
upon a new life. If the adopted person had children of his
own, as he well might have, these children also became
the children of the adopting father. The family was affected by the adoption just as much as the father was. In
Roman law the adopted person became in the most literal
sense the child of the adopting father. How literal this
sense was can be seen from the following case. Claudius,
the Roman Emperor, adopted Nero, so that Nero could
succeed him as Emperor. Nero was no relation. Claudius
already had a daughter called Octavia. It was thought that
Nero's succession would be still further assured if he mar-

ried Octavia. Nero and Octavia were not in any way blood relations, but in the eyes of the Roman law they were literally brother and sister because Claudius had adopted Nero; and the Roman senate had to pass a special bill before Nero could marry the girl, who was no relation to him, and who was yet in the eyes of the law his full sister.

It was of all this that Paul was thinking when he spoke of the adoption of the Christian into the family of God. The Christian received a new father—even God. The Christian's family were included with him; the promise was to his children also. All his past life was cancelled and there was given to him a new beginning and a new start, clean from the cancelled sins of the past. He became a full inheritor of the grace and the wealth of the riches of God. He became the kinsman of all the saints of God.

There is one more tremendous fact which is implied in this picture of adoption. So long as we think of religion in terms of law, and of the Christian as being under obligation to satisfy the law of God, then the relationship of the Christian to God is always that of slave to master, and of criminal to judge, and must always be a relationship compounded of distance and fear. But no sooner do we bring this idea of adoption into the picture at all than the relationship becomes a family relationship. By the very word adoption, God becomes Father, and we become child; and the very essence of religion becomes not a struggle to keep an impossible law, but the joy of entry, all undeserved, into the family of God.

IX

THE DEATH OF CHRIST

We have been looking at the great pictures which Paul used
to express the work of Jesus Christ; now we must turn our
thoughts to the most important of all parts of Paul's
thought. We must ask, for what did the death of Jesus
Christ stand in Paul's mind? Where does the Cross stand
in Paul's scheme of things?

One thing is certain—for Paul the Cross stood at the
centre of the Christian faith. Paul's unbroken insistence is
on the essential centrality of the Cross. He writes to the
Corinthians : " We preach Christ crucified " (*I Corinthians*
1.23). He writes : " I determined not to know any thing
among you, save Jesus Christ, and him crucified " (*I Corinthians* 2.2). He writes to the Galatians : " God forbid that
I should glory, save in the Cross of our Lord Jesus Christ "
(*Galatians* 6.14). There is no need to seek to prove that for
Paul the Cross of Christ stood in the centre of the universe.

It is further clear that to Paul the Cross of Christ had a
certain self-evidencing power. The Cross contained its own
appeal. To seek to decorate it with fine words was simply to
obscure it. To Paul the Cross was something to be shown to
men in all its stark simplicity. He will not preach with
wisdom of words lest the Cross of Christ should be made of
none effect (*I Corinthians* 1.17). He did not come with
excellency of speech or wisdom (*I Corinthians* 2.1). He cannot understand how the Galatians could have slipped back
when Christ had been placarded before their eyes (*Galatians* 3.1).

Paul would have said that first and foremost the Cross is
not something to be argued about, but something to be
shown to men. He had the conviction that the Cross has a
persuasive power of its own, that the story of the Cross
simply told will break the barriers down, that the first task

74

of the Christian preacher is without adornment to show to the world the Man upon the Cross. For that very reason it is all the more incumbent upon us to try to see what Paul saw in the death of Jesus Christ.

We may well begin with something about which there can be no possible dispute. Paul was quite certain that Jesus Christ died on behalf of men. We must be careful to get this phrase right. The preposition in the Greek is always *huper* which means *on behalf of*. The preposition is not *anti*, which would mean *instead of*. The Authorized Version usually translates it simply *for men*. We may very well find in the end that there is an element in Paul's thought that Jesus died in place of man, but the fundamental, basic essential thought is that Jesus died on the Cross on behalf of men. He writes to the Thessalonians of the Lord Jesus Christ who died for us (*I Thessalonians* 5.10). He pleads for consideration for the weaker brother for whom Christ died (*I Corinthians* 8.11). He talks of the brother for whom Christ died (*Romans* 14.15). He talks about Jesus Christ who loved the Church and gave himself for the Church (*Ephesians* 5.25). We may well begin with the simple and basic fact that Jesus Christ died on behalf of us, that his death achieved something for us that by ourselves we could never have achieved.

We may now go on to try to define more fully what this phrase *on behalf of* means and implies. Paul is clear that it was that death of Jesus Christ which achieved *reconciliation* between man and God. It is by the Cross and through the Cross that the relationship which should exist between man and God is restored. The gulf is bridged; the estrangement is healed; the enmity is taken away. He talks of us being reconciled to God by the death of his Son (*Romans* 5.10). He speaks of men being brought nigh by the blood of Christ (*Ephesians* 2.13). He speaks about God making peace by the blood of the Cross (*Colossians* 1.20). The death of Christ is that which achieved the reconciliation of man to God, that which restored the lost relationship of intimacy and of love.

We may pause to note that this in itself does not imply

or necessitate a substitutionary, or even in the narrower
sense, a sacrificial view of the death of Jesus Christ. Taken
by itself, apart from the other great sayings of Paul, it might
be interpreted to mean that the death of Christ gave men
such an utterly compelling demonstration of the love of God
that man is compelled to cease to see God as the lawgiver,
the taskmaster and the judge, and is compelled to begin to
see him as the lover of the souls of men. It might be interpreted to mean that the Cross says to men as nothing else in
the world does : God loves you like that, and that that discovery of the love of God was exactly the fact which produced this reconciliation which gave men peace with God.
There is indeed no possible doubt that that is part of Paul's
thought. " The love of Christ constraineth us," he said (*II
Corinthians* 5.14). There is no doubt that Paul did see in
the Cross a demonstration of that incredible and amazing
love, the sight of which could break the hearts of men. But
it would not be a fair reflection of the thought of Paul to
leave the matter there.

The thought of the Cross, the death of Jesus Christ, and
the idea of *redemption* are inextricably connected in the
mind of Paul. That emerges in a phrase so simple as : " The
Saviour, the Lord Jesus Christ " (*Philippians* 3.20). The
very use of the word *Saviour* makes it clear that there was
something from which man had to be saved and that that
salvation was wrought by the life and death of Jesus Christ.
In *Galatians* 4.5 Paul says quite plainly : " God sent forth
his Son . . . to redeem them that were under the law." In
such a phrase there must be two intertwined ideas. (*a*) God
sent his Son to rescue men from their bondage to the law, to
lead them away from that legalistic outlook which could result in nothing but estrangement from himself, to show them
that the dominant force in life must be, not law, but love.
(*b*) God sent his Son to save men from the penalties which
under law they had incurred. If there is a moral law in this
world, breach of that law must involve penalty; and God
sent his Son to rescue men from the situation into which
their sinning had brought them.

In *Ephesians* 1.7 Paul puts the two things together, as if

they were parallel. " In Jesus Christ we have redemption though his blood, the forgiveness of sins." The redemption is redemption from punishment which man has merited and deserved into a forgiveness and grace which he has not merited and which he has not deserved. The sentence is repeated word for word in *Colossians* 1.14. This redemption, liberation, emancipation, this gaining of freedom is something which has to be achieved by the paying of a price. It was the death of Jesus Christ which achieved this freedom; and it did so in a double way; it achieved present liberation and the blotting out of the handwriting which the sins of the past had produced against us (*Colossians* 2.14).

We must now approach the crucial essence of the matter. Over and over again Paul connects the death of Christ with *sin*. In this matter there are no hints and implications; the connection is definitely and bluntly made. The very first item of the belief which Paul received was that " Christ died for our sins according to the scriptures " (*I Corinthians* 15.3). He writes to the Galatians, at the very beginning of the letter, of Christ who gave himself for our sins (*Galatians* 1.4). He writes to the Romans of Jesus our Lord who was delivered for our offences (*Romans* 4.25). He says that in due time Christ died for the ungodly (*Romans* 5.6). He says that while we were yet sinners Christ died for us (*Romans* 5.8).

To Paul there was the clearest possible connection between the death of Jesus Christ and the sin of man. It was not only that the sin of man procured the death of Jesus Christ, although that was true; it was that the death of Christ did something to, and for, the sin of man.

It is necessary that we should pause here for a moment and gather up the materials as far as we have gone. We saw that for Paul the Cross has a strange self-evidencing power and that for him preaching consisted not in arguing about the Cross but in confronting men with the Cross. We saw that put in its very simplest form, Paul believed that Christ died on behalf of men. We saw that the great, basic work which Christ did on behalf of men was to reconcile them to God, that somehow his life, and especially his death, were effective in restoring the lost relationship between men and God. We saw that for Paul the death of Christ and the redemption, the liberation, the emancipation of men from the power and the penalty of sin are inextricably connected. Finally we saw that the death of Christ and the sin of man are bound up together; and we saw that it is not simply the sin of man which caused the death of Christ, but that the death of Christ did something to and for the sin of man.

There remains only one step to take, and in Pauline thought we must take it. Paul thought of the death of Jesus Christ in terms of *sacrifice*. In *Galatians* 2.20 he speaks of : " The Son of God, who loved me, and gave himself for me." In *Ephesians* 5.2 he used the actual word, for there he speaks of Christ " who loved us, and who gave himself for us an offering and a sacrifice to God ". Can we penetrate even more deeply into the meaning which Paul poured into this idea ?

There is one sentence in Paul's writings which may well give us the key and the clue to the whole of Paul's thought. In *I Corinthians* 5.7 Paul says : " Christ our Passover is sacrificed for us." What are we to read into, and to understand by, that phrase ? There are two possibilities.

The first is to take this phrase in a quite general way. The Passover was pre-eminently the feast which commemorated the deliverance of the people of Israel from bondage in the land of Egypt. The Passover Feast was designed to make it certain that the people of Israel would never forget that deliverance wrought for them by the hand of God. The phrase could therefore mean quite generally that the death of Jesus Christ is a sacrifice which has the effect of delivering men from the bondage to sin in which they are held. Truly that is a great and a true thought; but it may well be that in this phrase there is something more vivid and definite than that.

The essence of the Passover story lies in the name itself. The ancient story tells how the people of Israel were instructed to smear the lintels of their door with the blood of the lamb that had been slain; and when the angel, who had been sent to destroy the first-born son of every Egyptian home, saw that smear of blood, he would *pass over* that house (*Exodus* 12.22, 23). In later days, when they were asked the meaning of this feast, they were to say: "It is the sacrifice of the Lord's Passover, who passed over the houses of the children of Israel in Egypt when he smote the Egyptians, and delivered our houses" (*Exodus* 12.27). The essence of the Passover Feast, enshrined for ever in its very name, is the undying memory that the blood of the Passover lamb saved the inmates of the house from the visitation of death.

It is surely that idea that is in the mind of Paul. The death of Jesus Christ was that which saved men from the death in which their sins had involved them. If that is so—and we believe that for Paul it was so—then the death of Jesus Christ is in the most real sense a sacrifice for men, a sacrifice which saved them from the death of the soul which they had merited and deserved.

Paul makes two further statements which underline and stress that idea. They are sayings which emphasise the cost of salvation to Jesus Christ. In *Galatians* 3.13 he writes: "Christ hath redeemed us from the curse of the law, being made a curse for us: for it is written, Cursed is every one that hangeth on a tree." In *II Corinthians* 5.21 he writes: "For he hath made him to be sin for us, who knew no sin; that we might be made the righteousness of God in him." It is not possible to take these sayings as having any other meaning as Paul saw it, than that what ought to have happened to us did happen to Jesus Christ, and that he bore the suffering and the shame which we rightly should have done.

In any Jewish sin-offering, before the animal was sacrificed, the Jewish worshipper placed his hands on the victim's head and pressed on them, and then with penitence confessed his sin. The idea was that in some sense his sins were transferred to the animal, and the animal was a substitute for himself. Paul knew about all this. Without a doubt he must often have done all this; and at the end of it he was as far from God, and as estranged from him as ever. But the moment Christ came into his life, and the moment he was confronted with the Cross of Christ, then the barriers were removed, the estrangement was gone, the sense of separating guilt was taken away. For Paul Jesus Christ did that which all the sacrifices of Jewish ritual had failed to do; and, therefore, Paul saw in the death of Jesus Christ the supreme and the only availing sacrifice for the sin of men—and for his own sin.

One of the most famous passages in *The Pilgrim's Progress* is the passage where John Bunyan tells how Christian lost his burden : " Now I saw in my dream that the highway up which Christian was to go was fenced on either side with a wall, and that wall was called Salvation. Up this way, therefore, did burdened Christian run, but not without great difficulty, because of the burden on his back. He ran thus till he came to a place somewhat ascending, and upon that place stood a cross, and a little below, in the bottom, a sepulchre. So I saw in my dream, that just as Christian came up with the cross, his burden loosed from off his shoulders, and fell from off his back, and began to tumble, and so continued to do, till it came to the mouth of the sepulchre, where it fell in, and I saw it no more." For Bunyan, as for Paul, the Cross removed for ever the burden of sin.

We can now go back and read all Paul's pictures in the light of the sacrifice of the Cross.

There is *Justification,* the picture from the law courts. God treats the sinner as if he had been a good man, and welcomes him as if he had never been away. But the fact remains that sin must have its punishment; if God is to be true to himself, sin cannot be dismissed as something which does not matter, or there arises moral chaos; therefore, someone must have paid the penalty which was due; and that someone was Jesus Christ. We are, as Paul put it, justified by his blood (*Romans* 5.9).

There is *Reconciliation,* the picture from friendship. But the fact remains that no one can draw near to the holiness of God, unless he has clean hands and a pure heart, for God in his very nature is of purer eyes than to behold iniquity.

Someone must supply the merits which are necessary for that approach; and that someone is Jesus Christ.

There is *Redemption, Emancipation,* the picture from slavery. It is true that man is delivered from the bondage of sin, but no man, in a world of slavery, ever received his freedom unless he paid the price, or unless some generous-hearted soul paid it for him, when he could not pay it for himself. Man's emancipation had its cost; man's freedom had its price; someone had to pay that cost and that price and that someone was Jesus Christ.

There is *Adoption,* the picture from the family. The whole of the adoption ceremony in Roman law centred on the moment when the adopted person passed from one *patria potestas* to another, the moment when he received a new father. But again that ceremony centred in a symbolic sale; someone had to pay the price, and that someone was Jesus Christ.

There is *Propitiation,* the picture from sacrifice. According to Jewish religion, for every sin there was the necessary sacrifice which was the sign and the guarantee of the true penitence of the man who brought it. But Paul's experience was that there was no such thing as a human sacrifice of any animal, however costly, which removed the feeling of guilt and atoned for sin. Such a sacrifice had to be found, if man was ever to be at peace with God; and on his Cross Jesus Christ made and paid that sacrifice.

There is one last picture which Paul uses. It is a picture which is seldom talked about nowadays; but in view of all that we have said it is very close to the heart of Paul. It is the metaphor from the world of *accounting.* It is in the word *logizesthai,* which the Authorized Version translates *to count* or *to impute* or *to reckon (Romans* 4.3, 5, 6, 8, 9, 10, 11). The word *logizesthai* means *to set down to some-one's account.* It can be used equally of setting down to a man's debit or to a man's credit.

Paul's idea is that there is not a man in all the world who has not a vast debit balance in his account with God; he is in God's debt to an extent that he can never pay. But, in the mercy of God, his debt is cancelled and the merits of Jesus are credited to him, and he is clothed with a righteousness which is not his own. To take a very distant analogy—we are sometimes allowed entry into a group or a society or a house, not because of any qualifications of our own, but because of the qualifications of the friend who introduces us. So we are welcomed into the presence of God, not because of anything we are, or can bring, or can do, but because of the merits of Jesus Christ who introduces us into the presence and the family of God.

Paul saw in the death of Jesus Christ an action of God himself, by which God made it possible for the sinner to come home to him, and possible for himself to accept that sinner when he came.

X

THE RISEN CHRIST

To anyone who reads the Book of Acts with even the most cursory attention it is immediately clear that the early Church was characteristically and specifically the Church of the Risen Christ. At that stage the attention of the Church was focused on the Resurrection even more than it was upon the Cross.

There was a reason for that. At that time the Church was still mainly Jewish. Because of that, men were still thinking of Jesus in terms of Jewish Messiahship; and the one thing which was the final guarantee that Jesus was the Messiah was the fact that he had risen from the dead. It was inevitable and right that at that stage the attention of men should be fixed upon the Resurrection.

It is true that in the writings and the thought of Paul the emphasis to some degree changes. It is true that Paul's emphasis is on the Cross, and on the atoning and sacrificial death of Jesus Christ. But to the end of the day it remains true that for Paul, as for the early Church as a whole, the Resurrection was central to the christian faith.

When we read the Synoptic Gospels and hear the actual words of Jesus, we find that Jesus never foretold his death without foretelling his rising again. He never thought of the shame without the triumph. The humiliation and the glory were integrally and inseparably connected. The one could not exist without the other. It is Jesus' first announcement of his death to his disciples that, "The Son of Man must suffer many things, and be rejected of the elders, and of the chief priests, and scribes, and be killed, and after three days rise again" (*Mark* 8.31; cp. *Mark* 9.31). To Jesus the Cross and the Resurrection were part of the same process and he could never speak of the Cross without speaking of the triumph which lay beyond it.

83

It was the same with Paul. He speaks of Jesus Christ "who was delivered for our offences and raised again for our justification" (*Romans* 4.25). He says that though Jesus Christ "was crucified through weakness, yet he liveth by the power of God" (*II Corinthians* 13.4). In the great *Philippians* passage (*Philippians* 2.5-11) the humiliation of Jesus Christ is set out in all its stark terribleness, but the passage comes to its triumphant conclusion: "wherefore God also hath highly exalted him." Paul was like his Master; he could never speak of the agony and the shame of the Cross without his thoughts going beyond it to the triumph and the splendour of the Resurrection.

How central the thought of the Resurrection was to Paul may be seen from the fact that he mentions it specifically in every letter except *II Thessalonians* and *Philemon*; and even in those two letters, although the fact of the Resurrection is not definitely stated, the thought of the Risen Christ still permeates all things.

He writes to the Romans: "Like as Christ was raised from the dead by the glory of the Father, even so we also should walk in newness of life" (*Romans* 6.4; cp. 7.4). To the Corinthians he writes: "God hath both raised up the Lord, and will raise up us by his own power" (*I Corinthians* 6.14; cp. *II Corinthians* 13.4). His very first words to the Galatians are of "Jesus Christ, and God the Father, who raised him from the dead" (*Galatians* 1.1). To the Philippians he writes that God "has highly exalted him, and given him a name which is above every name" (*Philippians* 2.9). To the Ephesians he writes of the power of God "which he wrought in Christ, when he raised him from the dead" (*Ephesians* 1.20). To the Colossians he writes of "God, who has raised Christ from the dead" (*Colossians* 2.12). Paul could not think of Jesus Christ without thinking of him as the Saviour who died and the Lord who rose again.

This is very important, for from Paul we learn that the fact of the Resurrection was an essential part of the teaching of the early Church. It is to be remembered that the writings of Paul take us back to a time before the writing of the gospels. It is most probably true to say that none of the gospels, as we know them, had come into being before the last of Paul's letters was written. Certainly, if they were in existence, they were not widespread and universally accepted documents of the christian faith. But there was in existence a body of oral tradition. In an age in which books were few and hand-written and printing had not yet been invented, it was in fact by oral tradition that truth and history were commonly handed down. Very early this oral tradition was stereotyped and crystallized. It was the basis of instruction for those who were entering the Church for the first time; it was the essential raw material of all the teaching and the preaching of the Church; and certainly it was the concentrated essence of the teaching of the first missionaries wherever they went. An essential element in that first universal tradition was the story and the facts of the Resurrection.

In *I Corinthians* 15 Paul has his fullest teaching about the Resurrection. He begins with the facts of the Resurrection, and his first word is: " I delivered unto you first of all that which I also received " (*I Corinthians* 15.3). When he told the story of the Resurrection, he passed on the standard teaching of the Church. This is important, for it means that the story of the Resurrection is not a late and a legendary development and embroidery of the christian story, but that it was embodied in it from the very first moment of the christian Church.

But to the evidence of the tradition of the Church, Paul has something to add—the evidence of his own experience. He gives his list of the Resurrection appearances of Jesus, and then he says: " And last of all he was seen by me also, as of one born out of due time " (*I Corinthians* 15.8). For Paul the Resurrection was not a story which he had to accept at second hand and on the evidence of someone else. It was something which he had experienced, something of which he could give an eye-witness account, something for which his evidence was independent and at first hand.

There can have been no time when the Church did not possess something in the nature of a creed, however bare and summary that brief statement of the faith must have been. The Church existed in the midst of a pagan society, and it must always have been able briefly and succinctly to tell that pagan society where it stood. In a Church into which converts from heathenism were pouring in a constant flood, it must always have been necessary to have some brief statement of the faith, which converts on baptism could publicly confess. We learn from Paul that the fact of the Resurrection was an absolutely essential part of that first creed, and of that earliest public confession. In *Romans* 10.9 we read : " If thou shalt confess with thy mouth the Lord Jesus, and shalt believe in thine heart that God hath raised him from the dead, thou shalt be saved." Clearly that sentence is an extract or an echo from the confession of faith and creed of the early Church, an echo of the simple statement on which the early Christians took their stand. We can therefore clearly see that the Resurrection is not only an integral part of early Church tradition, but that it was also an essential part of the first creed, and an essential element in the first confession of faith. It is true to say that the Church itself, and the faith of each individual Christian within it, is founded on belief in the Risen Christ. This is not a late development which was added to the Church's faith, it is there from the very beginning. It was in fact the foundation stone of the Church's faith.

Before we begin to see more of what the Resurrection meant to Paul, we must note one basic fact. For Paul, in the plainest and most literal sense, the Resurrection was an act of God. It is true that sometimes Paul does say that Jesus rose from the dead; but far oftener he says that God raised Jesus from the dead. For Paul the Resurrection is the product of the power of God, the act of the hand of God. He speaks of God who raised up Jesus our Lord from the dead (*Romans* 4.24). He says that God has raised up the Lord (*I Corinthians* 6.14). When Paul speaks of the Resurrection, his characteristic way of speaking of it is as an act of God. The Resurrection was in fact the complete and final and unanswerable demonstration of the indestructible and undefeatable power of God.

There was one mistake into which the early Church was never in any danger of falling. In those early days men never thought of Jesus Christ as a figure in a book. They never thought of him as someone who had lived and died, and whose story was told and passed down in history, as the story of someone who had lived and whose life had ended. They did not think of him as someone who had been but as someone who is. They did not think of Jesus Christ as someone whose teaching must be discussed and debated and argued about; they thought of him as someone whose presence could be enjoyed and whose constant fellowship could be experienced. Their faith was not founded on a book; their faith was founded on a person.

The whole aim of Paul and early Church was not to tell men about Jesus Christ, but to introduce them to Jesus Christ, and his presence and his power. In the early days— as it should be now—Christianity was not argument about a dead person, however great; it was encounter with a living presence.

We must now go on to see something of what that fact of the Resurrection meant to Paul.

The Resurrection was to Paul the final proof that Jesus was the Messiah. In one case he quite definitely says that. In *Romans* 1.4 he speaks of Jesus Christ " declared to be the Son of God with power . . . by the resurrection from the dead ".

It was inevitable that the Jews should think of Jesus in terms of Messiahship. Always they had been waiting for the Messiah of God. Inevitably they had thought of the Messiah in terms of glory, of conquest, and of power. But in Jesus they were confronted with a Messiah who had died upon a Cross. Something tremendous was needed to convince them that this man, who contradicted all the accepted ideas of Messiahship was indeed the chosen one of God. That one convincing fact was the Resurrection, for the Resurrection was a triumph and a glory beyond any triumph of which men had ever dreamed.

It may be wondered why Paul does not make more of this idea. When he does state it, he states it very definitely;

but he does not turn to it very often. The reason is that, for the most part, Paul was dealing with Gentiles in his letters, and this idea was an idea which was more relevant to a Jew than to a Gentile. But we do know that, when Paul preached to Jews, he did use this idea as a main part of his preaching. We have in *Acts* 13.14-43 Luke's account of a sermon of Paul in the Synagogue at Antioch in Pisidia; and in that sermon Paul does seek to convince the Jews of the Messiahship of Jesus by the fact of the Resurrection. To a Jew the fact of the Resurrection was the proof that, in spite of the way in which the Cross contradicted the accepted idea of Messiahship, Jesus really and truly was The Anointed One of God.

The idea of the Risen Christ as the perfect High Priest is an idea which is characteristic of the Letters to the Hebrews. But once at least Paul uses that idea. In *Romans* 8.27 he speaks of the Risen Christ making intercession for the saints according to the will of God; and in *Romans* 8.34 he speaks of Christ being at the right hand of God, and also making intercession for us. Paul saw in the Risen Christ the one who even in the heavenly places is still pleading the cause of men, and still opening the door to the presence of God for men.

The word priest has gained at least in some minds a meaning which it ought never to have had. To some minds the word priest suggests a person who shuts men off from God, who bars the way to God, who with his ritual and his claims comes between men and God. But the Latin word for priest is *pontifex,* which means a *bridge-builder;* and a real priest is a man who builds a bridge between his fellowmen and God. Even in heaven the Risen Church as Paul saw it, is still doing the work he did on earth; he is still opening the way for men to God.

The idea of the Risen Christ as Judge is another idea which occurs in the thought of Paul. It appears in *Romans* 14.9, 10. " For to this end Christ both died, and rose, and revived, that he might be the Lord both of the dead and living. But why dost thou judge thy brother, or why dost thou set at nought thy brother? we shall all stand before the judgment seat of Christ." That same Jesus, on whom men sat in judgment and who was condemned by men, is the Risen Christ before whose judgment seat all men must appear.

There is one idea which is very deeply rooted in the mind of Paul, and very near and dear to his heart. That is the idea of the power of the Resurrection. In *Philippians* 3.10 Paul describes one of the supreme aims of his life as " to know the power of His Resurrection ". In *Ephesians* 1.19, 20 he speaks of the greatness of God's power to us who believe, that power which was operative in the Resurrection.

Again and again Paul connects the Resurrection with the new life which the Christian is enabled to lead, and the new goodness which clothes the Christian man. In *Romans* 6.4 he says that, just as Christ was raised from the dead, by the glory of the Father, " even so we also should walk in newness of life ". In *Romans* 7.4 he says that Jesus Christ was raised from the dead that " we should bring forth fruit unto God ". In *Colossians* 2.12 he speaks of the Resurrection and goes straight on to speak of the christian forgiveness of sins and triumph over sins. In *II Corinthians* 13.4 he tells how Christ was crucified in his human weakness, but lives by the power of God; and then he goes on to say that " we also are weak in him, but we shall live with him by the power of God toward you ".

Paul saw in the Resurrection a release of divine power, a surging tide of power which cleansed and beautified the life of the Christian. To Paul the Resurrection was not a past fact, but a present power.

There is no incomprehensible, mystic mystery here. If Christ is risen from the dead, it means that it is possible for the Christian to live every moment of every day in the presence and the fellowship of the living Christ. It means that the Christian approaches no tasks alone, bears no sorrow alone, attacks no problem alone, faces no demand alone, endures no temptation alone. It means that Jesus Christ does not issue his commands, and then leave us to do our best to obey them alone, but that he is constantly with us to enable us to perform that which he commands.

There is a very beautiful saying of Christ which is one of the unwritten sayings which do not appear in the New Testament at all : " Raise the stone and you will find me; cleave the wood and I am there." It means that, as the mason works at the stone, as the carpenter handles the wood, the Risen Christ is with him. The Resurrection means that every way of life can be walked hand in hand with the living Christ. The reservoir of the power of his presence is open for every Christian to draw upon.

But the most uncompromising statement of the utter necessity of the Resurrection is in *I Corinthians* 15.14-19. There Paul writes : " If Christ be not risen, then is our preaching vain, and your faith is also vain . . . If Christ be not raised, your faith is vain; ye are yet in your sins. Then they also which are fallen asleep in Christ are perished. If in this life only we have hope in Christ, we are of all men most miserable." Why should that be so? What are the great truths which the Resurrection, and the Resurrection alone, guarantees and conserves? The Resurrection is the guarantee of four great truths.

It proves that *truth is stronger than falsehood.* In Jesus Christ God's truth came to men; men sought to eliminate, to obliterate, to destroy that truth, but the Resurrection is the final proof of the indestructibility of the truth of God.

It proves that *good is stronger than evil.* Jesus Christ was the incarnate goodness of God. The sin of man sought to destroy that goodness. But the Resurrection is the proof that goodness must in the end triumph over all that evil can do to it.

It is proof that *life is stronger than death.* Men sought to destroy the life of Jesus Christ once and for all; the Resurrection is the proof that the life which is in Christ cannot be destroyed—and the Christian shares that life.

It is the proof that *love is stronger than hate.* In the last analysis the contest in Jerusalem was a contest between the hatred of men and the love of God. Men took that love and sought to break it for ever on the Cross; but the Resurrection is the proof that the love of God is stronger than all the hatred of men, and can in the end defeat all that that hatred can do to it.

Unless we could be certain of these great truths life would be intolerable.

To Paul the Resurrection of Jesus Christ was neither simply a fact in history nor a theological dogma. It was the supreme fact of experience. To Paul the fact of the Resurrection meant the greatest thing in all the world; it meant that all life is lived in the presence of the love and of the power of Jesus Christ.

XI

IN CHRIST

Every man who writes or speaks a great deal has favourite phrases. He uses them almost without knowing that he is doing so. Paul had such a phrase, and the phrase is *in Christ*. We have been studying something of what Jesus Christ meant to Paul, and it is fitting that now we should turn to this phrase, which occurs so often in Paul's writings and which clearly meant so much to him.

This phrase is not so much the essence of Paul's theology, as it is the summary of his whole religion. For Paul this phrase *in Christ* was always a compendious statement of the Christian faith. Of all the letters which Paul ever wrote, it is absent only in one—in *II Thessalonians*. No one would deny that the passing of the years deepened and enriched and intensified its meaning for Paul; but the fact remains that this phrase and all that it means was no late and sudden development in the mind and thought and heart of Paul. From the beginning to the end of his christian life it was the centre and soul of his christian experience.

Still further, we must note that Paul never at any time looked on this phrase as describing a religious experience which was unique and peculiar to himself. It was not something which he enjoyed because he was in a specially privileged position, or because he had risen to a devotional height, which ordinary people could never hope to scale. It was something to be known and experienced by every Christian man and woman. Paul would not only have said that the phrase *in Christ* was the essence of the christian life in general; he would have said that it is the essence of every individual christian life also.

Still further yet, we must note that Paul never uses the phrase *in Jesus*; he talks about being *in Christ, in Christ Jesus, in Jesus Christ, in the Lord*, but never *in Jesus*. That is to say, this phrase has to do uniquely and specifically with the Risen Christ. It does not describe or express a physical relationship, which is dependent on space and time and physical contact, a relationship which can be found and lost as presence and absence alternate. It describes a spiritual relationship, which is independent of space and time, a relationship of the ever and everywhere present Risen Lord and everliving Christ. Tennyson came near to expressing it when he wrote in *The Higher Pantheism* :

Speak to him thou for he hears, and Spirit with Spirit can meet—
Closer is he than breathing, and nearer than hands and feet.

This is not a necessarily limited relationship with a physical person; it is an unlimited relationship with the Risen Lord.

We must begin by going to the letters of Paul, and examining in some detail how he uses this phrase *in Christ*.

Paul thought of the Church as a whole, and of each of the Churches, as being in Christ. The Church in Thessalonica is in God and in the Lord Jesus Christ (*I Thessalonians* 1.1). The Churches of Judæa are in Christ (*Galatians* 1.22). The individual Churches may be in different and widely separated parts of the world; but they are all in Christ. The life of the Church is life in Christ.

But not only are the Churches in Christ; the individual members of the Churches, the individual Christians are in Christ. *Philippians* is addressed to the saints in Christ Jesus who are at Philippi (*Philippians* 1.1). Greetings are sent to every saint in Christ Jesus (*Philippians* 4.21). The members of the Church at Philippi are brethren in the Lord (*Philippians* 1.14). The letter to Colosse is addressed to the saints and faithful brethren in Christ who are at Colosse (*Colossians* 1.2). When Epaphroditus is sent back to Philippi after his serious illness in Rome, he is to be received in the Lord (*Philippians* 2.29). Those who are set in authority in the Church are over the others in the Lord (*I Thessalonians* 5.12).

The fact that all individual Christians are in Christ is indeed precisely the source and origin of that unity which

should characterise all members of the Church. All Christians are the children of God by faith in Christ Jesus (*Galatians* 3.26) and because of that circumcision and uncircum-
cision are irrelevant (*Galatians* 5.6). In Christ there is
neither Jew nor Greek, male nor female, bond nor free
(*Galatians* 3.28). All Christians are one body in Christ
(*Romans* 12.5). It is God's aim to bring unity to a disintegrated universe and that unity can only come in Christ
(*Ephesians* 1.10). This must operate in the most practical
way. The two women in Philippi who have quarrelled are
urged to come together again in Christ (*Philippians* 4.2).
Because every Church is in Christ, there can never be disunity between real Churches. Because every Christian is in
Christ, there can never be any barrier between those who
are truly Christian. They may be of different nations and
colours and status and class and ability and rank and birth;
they may belong to different branches of the Church; they
may differ in language, in politics, in methods, in ritual, in
liturgy, in administration; these differences do not, and
cannot, matter, if men and women are in Christ.

The disunities of the Church would be solved tomorrow,
if men realised that Christianity does not mean being in a
Church, but being in Christ.

For Paul himself life was lived in Christ. Every action
which he did, every word which he spoke, every experience
which he underwent was in Christ. His ways are in Christ
(*I Corinthians* 4.17). He has begotten the Corinthians in
Christ, and they are his work in the Lord (*I Corinthians*
4.15; 9.1). He speaks in Christ (*II Corinthians* 2.17; 12.19).
He makes his plans and thinks of the future in Christ. In
the Lord he trusts to send Timothy to Philippi, and in the
Lord he trusts soon to come himself (*Philippians* 2.19, 24).
He sends his love to the Corinthians in Christ (*I Corin-
thians* 16.24). In speaking of himself and of his own
spiritual experience, he says that he knows a man in Christ
(*II Corinthians* 12.2). Even in prison his bonds are in
Christ (*Philippians* 1.13).

It is not only Paul who can write like this. Tertius, the
amanuensis who wrote *Romans* to Paul's dictation, sends

his greeting in the Lord (*Romans* 16.22). It is open to any Christian to enter into that relationship with Christ in which his whole life will be in Christ.

It is, in fact, the case that at least sometimes *in Christ* simply means *Christian* in the real and deepest sense of the term. *Romans* 16 is specially instructive in this direction. In that chapter the phrase *in Christ* occurs no fewer than nine times in the compass of fifteen verses. Phoebe is to be received in the Lord (verse 2); she is to be given a true christian welcome. Priscilla and Aquila are Paul's helpers in Christ Jesus (verse 3); they are his helpers in all christian work and activity. Andronicus and Junia were in Christ before Paul (verse 7); they were Christians before Paul was. Amplias is my beloved in the Lord (verse 8); he is the fellow-Christian whom Paul loved. Urbane is our helper in Christ; that is, our helper in christian work (verse 9). Apelles is approved in Christ (verse 10); he is a well-proved Christian. The household of Narcissus are in the Lord (verse 11); they are Christians. Tryphena and Tryphosa labour in the Lord (verse 12); they are engaged actively in christian work. Persis laboured in the Lord and Rufus was chosen in the Lord (verse 13); Persis is engaged in christian work, and Rufus was chosen as a Christian by Jesus Christ himself. It can be seen that in nearly all these cases the phrase *in Christ,* or its equivalent, could be translated Christian, although that would be a colourless and inadequate translation.

As Paul saw it, all great christian gifts and all great christian qualities are in Christ. We have consolation in Christ (*Philippians* 2.1). We are bold in Christ (*Philemon* 8). We have liberty in Christ (*Galatians* 2.4). We have truth in Christ (*Romans* 9.1). We have the promise in Christ (*Ephesians* 3.6). The promises of God are confirmed and guaranteed in Christ (*II Corinthians* 1.20). We are sanctified in Christ (*I Corinthians* 1.2). We are wise in Christ (*I Corinthians* 4.10). We are new creatures in Christ (*II Corinthians* 5.17). We are called in the Lord (*I Corinthians* 7.22). The high calling of God is in Christ (*Philippians* 3.14). We are babes in Christ (*I Corinthians* 3.1).

God has stablished us in Christ (*II Corinthians* 1.21). We walk in Christ (*Colossians* 2.6).

It can be seen that for Paul the whole process and itinerary of the christian life is in Christ. The call to it is in Christ; we begin by being babes in Christ; we are stablished in Christ; the gifts of nurture and of strength are in Christ; the christian way is walked in Christ. For Paul the christian life is begun, continued and ended in Christ.

But special occasions and special demands and special crises demand special powers and gifts, and these special powers and gifts come to us in Christ.

In times of persecution and of peril it is in the Lord that Christians stand fast (*I Thessalonians* 3.8; *Philippians* 4.1). It is in Christ that we find joy in times of sorrow (*Philippians* 1.26; 3.1; 4.4; 4.10). It is in Christ that his servants are faithful. So Timothy is faithful in the Lord (*I Corinthians* 4.17); and the letter to the Ephesians is addressed to those who are faithful in the Lord (*Ephesians* 1.1).

Every good thing that we have experienced, that we possess and enjoy, that we can attain, is in Christ. In the letter to Philemon Paul speaks of every good thing which is in you in Christ (*Philemon* 6); and in Ephesians he speaks of God who has blessed us with all spiritual blessings in Christ (*Ephesians* 1.3).

There is one way in which it might be possible to simplify the whole matter. The phrase in Greek is *en Christō*. In classical Greek *en* does mean *in*; but in the later Greek of New Testament times *en* is very often commonly used of the *instrument* or *agent*, and very often means *by means of*, or *through the agency of*. Linguistically, it would be possible to take the phrase *en Christō* to mean *through Christ*, *by means of Christ*, *through the agency of Christ*. The phrase would then mean that Christ is the enabling power; that it is through his grace and power that we are enabled to live the christian life. It would be simple to think of being called by Christ; of standing fast in persecution and peril through the help that Christ gives; of receiving wisdom and truth through the agency of Christ.

To take *en Christō* in this sense, certainly in many cases, gives us a perfectly intelligible meaning; and he who looks for easy solutions, and who is impatient of anything that has any kind of mysticism in it, may well be tempted to accept the meaning; but the fact is that in many passages we will be compelled to admit that *en Christō* means far more than this. That key might unlock some doors, but it certainly would not unlock all the doors; and the doors it did unlock would lead us to the ante-chambers and the vestibule of the treasure-house which lies beyond. To say that the phrase *in Christ* means *through Christ* is true, but considerably less than half the truth.

It might be possible to argue that this phrase could be taken in a purely metaphorical sense. We could cite as some kind of parallel or analogy such a phrase as being wrapped up in a person. When two people are very near and dear to each other, when they are very intimate, when they love each other, and are interested only in each other, we can and do talk of them as being wrapped up in each other. There is no doubt that this line of thought does throw a ray of light on this matter, because it is a metaphor taken from the sphere of love, and it is only in the sphere of love that we can express Paul's relationship to Christ at all. But the cumulative effect of all Paul's uses of the phrase *in Christ* demands something even more than this. Something even more intimate and certainly more lasting is expressed by the phrase *in Christ*.

There are some who would go to the pagan religious background of Paul's time for the explanation of this phrase. In Paul's time the outstanding religious phenomenon of the Graeco-Roman world was the Mystery Religions. These Mystery Religions were based on what we would call passion plays. Their central act was the dramatic presentation of a story of some god who lived and suffered and died and rose again. Greek mythology was full of stories like that. Before the initiate was allowed to be present at such a performance he or she had to undergo a long process of training and instruction and fasting and asceticism; the person to be initiated was worked up to a high pitch of emotional excitement and expectation. The

performance itself was given under conditions carefully cal-
culated to drive a person to a kind of hysterical ecstasy.
Cunning lighting, perfumed incense, sensuous music were
all used to heighten the emotional atmosphere; and the aim
of the whole process and presentation was to enable the
worshipper to experience a complete identification with the
god whose story was being played out. The worshipper
became one with the god, sharing his sufferings, his death
and his final triumphant resurrection, till in the end the
worshipper could and did say : " I am thou, and thou art
I."

Beyond a doubt men did undergo an amazing experience
in the Mystery Religions. But there are two reasons why
this will not do as an explanation of the phrase *in Christ*.
First, the experience of the Mystery Religions was ecstatic,
hysterical, highly emotional. But there is nothing emotional
and ecstatic in the experience which Paul summarises in the
phrase *in Christ*. To be in Christ was not a brief ecstasy,
induced by deliberately provoked psychological excitement;
it was something which was obtained every day in the
ordinary business and routine of everyday life. Second, the
experience of the Mystery Religions was necessarily tran-
sient. It might be very vivid in the brief moment of ecstasy;
it might be repeated again under favourable circumstances;
but the experience which Paul describes in the phrase *in
Christ* is something which is lasting and permanent, something which endures, not for one exotic hour, but for a lifetime of day-to-day living.

We will not find the explanation of Paul's *in Christ* in
the Mystery Religions, although the experience they offered
may well have been a dim foretaste of the christian reality.

Deissmann suggested that this phrase can be interpreted
by using the analogy of the way in which we live in the air.
Just as all men live in the air, and cannot live without the
air, so the Christian lives in Christ. And just as the air is
inside all living things, in a man's lungs and in a man's
body, so Christ is in the man. Just as all men live in the
air, so the Christian lives in Christ; just as the air within
them gives all men life, so Christ within him gives the

Christian newness of life. To be in Christ is to live a life in which Christ is the atmosphere which we breathe. That is undoubtedly a lovely thought, and yet it has in it a nebulousness which is not in the Pauline conception.

There are certain other pictures which Paul uses about the christian experience of Christ, which will enable us to come nearer to the meaning of his phrase *in Christ*.

(*a*) In *Galatians* 3.27 he says that those who have been baptised into Christ have put on Christ; and in *Romans* 13.14 he tells his Roman friends : " Put ye on the Lord Jesus Christ." It is as if the Christian is encompassed, enveloped, clothed with Christ as he is with his clothes.

(*b*) In *Galatians* 4.19 he has a vivid picture. "My little children," he says, "of whom I travail in birth again until Christ be formed in you." In the christian life, Jesus Christ is born into a man, until the man is filled with the life of Christ.

(*c*) In *Galatians* 2.20 there is the great passage : "I am crucified with Christ; nevertheless I live; yet not I, but Christ liveth in me." The life principle which was Paul is dead; and Christ has become the life principle in him. The self of Paul is dead, and in its place Christ lives in him.

(*d*) Most vivid of all is the picture of baptism in *Romans* 6 and in *Colossians* 2.12. We have to remember that baptism was adult baptism, because it was the reception into the Church of men and women coming straight from paganism; and we have to remember that it was by total immersion. What the *Romans* 6 passage is saying is : When a man is immersed in the water, it is like going down into the grave and being buried and dying once and for all. When he emerges from the water, it is as if he emerged a new person, with a new life in him, and that new life is Christ.

Let us remember who and what Paul was. Once he had been a persecutor, pillaging the Church as a marauding army pillaged a city, as a wild boar laid waste a vineyard. Then on the Damascus Road something happened. In one flash of time, Paul the enemy of Christ became Paul the slave of Christ. It is difficult to describe it any other way than to say that in that moment one man died and another man was born. The old Paul was dead and a new Paul was born. And who had been responsible for this change? None other than the Risen Christ. From that moment Paul felt that between him and Christ there was so real, so close, so indissoluble a union that it could not be expressed in any other way than to say that he lived in Christ, and Christ lived in him.

It was not a case of identification with Christ; Paul did not lose his own personality; for Paul could still kneel and look up and worship and adore. But something had happened which brought Christ into Paul's heart and joined Paul's life to the life of Christ in such a way that he could only say that he was for ever in Christ.

We are here trying to describe something which has to be experienced to be understood. It has been said with the greatest truth that Christianity can only be understood from the inside. To the vast majority of people Paul's experience must remain a mystery—and the reason is that no man can enjoy Paul's experience of Christ, unless he has made Paul's surrender to Christ. It is only the completely surrendered heart which knows what it is to be in Christ in the fullest sense of the term.

XII

PAUL'S CONCEPTION OF FAITH

It is quite clear that there is no word so near the centre of Paul's belief as the word faith. We have only to read his letters to see that for Paul the word faith sums up the very essence of Christianity. It is therefore of supreme importance that we should understand something of what Paul meant by faith, if we are to understand what Christianity meant to him.

It is of primary importance to note that for Paul faith is always faith in a person. Faith is not the intellectual acceptance of a body of doctrine; faith is faith in a person. Sanday and Headlam have laid it down that there are four main meanings of the word faith, and four main connections in which Paul uses it—belief in God, belief in Jesus, belief in the promises of God, and belief in the promises of Jesus. It is indeed probable that all the Pauline usages of the word faith could be fitted into that scheme; but it will be even more illuminating to go direct to the letters themselves, and to examine the way in which Paul uses the word faith in them.

We must begin with a meaning which is not theological at all, and which needs no special background of expert knowledge to understand it. Paul uses faith to mean loyalty, fidelity, that which we would more naturally call faithfulness. That is the way in which he uses this word faith when he is talking of the fruit of the Spirit (*Galatians* 5.22). There faith is simply loyalty and the fidelity which are the most valuable qualities in life. Paul writes regularly to his Churches of the gratitude with which he had heard of their faith, and of the praise which their faith has won them. He says that the faith of the Roman Church is spoken of throughout the world (*Romans* 1.8). In *Ephesians* 1.15 he says that he has heard of the faith of those to whom he writes. In *Colossians* 1.4 he tells the Colossians that he has heard of their faith; and he speaks of the steadfastness of their faith in Christ (*Colossians* 2.5). He writes to the Thessalonians that the story of their faith has penetrated not only over all Macedonia, but even throughout the whole province of Achaia (*I Thessalonians* 1.8). He tells them that, since he had to leave them hurriedly and secretly, he now writes to inquire about their faith (*I Thessalonians* 3.5). He speaks of their patience and their faith (*II Thessalonians* 1.4). He writes to the Philippians of the sacrifice and service of their faith (*Philippians* 2.17).

In all these cases the reference is to the loyalty and the fidelity of the young Churches to Jesus Christ, a loyalty and a fidelity which overcame persecution and shone through the darkness of the troubled life which the early Christians had to lead.

Plainest of all cases of this meaning is *Romans* 3.3. There Paul contrasts the faithlessness of Israel with the faithfulness of God. Shall their unbelief, he demands, make the faith of God of no effect? What he means is that not all the disobedience, the unresponsiveness, the rebelliousness of man, can alter the fidelity of God to his purposes and to his promises. It is exactly the same in *I Thessalonians* 3.6 where Paul says that he has received good news of their faith. His information is that they are standing fast.

The Second Book of Samuel has a moving instance of this fidelity (*II Samuel* 15.19-23). David had fallen on evil days. Absalom his son had turned against him and the hearts of the people had gone out after Absalom. For David nothing but flight was left. Amongst his bodyguard David had a soldier called Ittai, who was a soldier of fortune. Ittai was not even an Israelite; he was a Philistine; he was one of those men who fought for the love of fighting, a mercenary who would sell his sword to the highest bidder. David saw that Ittai was preparing to follow him into exile and misfortune, and he told Ittai that he was under no obligation to come with him. He was a stranger and a foreigner; there was no call on him to involve his fortunes with the fallen

fortunes of David. Ittai answered : "As the lord liveth, and
as my lord the king liveth, surely in what place my lord the
king shall be, whether in death or life, even there also will
thy servant be." That is precisely what Paul meant by faith
at its simplest. Faith at its simplest is unshakable and unalterable loyalty to Jesus Christ.

Closely connected with this is the idea of faith as belief,
the unalterable conviction that certain things are true. Paul
writes to the Corinthians that their faith should not stand by
wisdom (*I Corinthians* 2.5). The meaning is that their belief
in the power of Christianity, their conviction that Jesus
Christ is Lord, should not be something which is dependent
on and bolstered up by fine-spun and rhetorical human
arguments. In *I Corinthians* 15.17 he says that if Christ is
not risen from the dead, then their faith is vain. That is to
say, if there is no Resurrection, then all their convictions
have collapsed, the bottom is knocked out of all that they
have accepted as true.

There were two stages in the religious life of John
Bunyan. At first he could only say that the Jews think
their religion the best, and the Mohammedans think their
religion the best, and ask : "What if Christianity be but a
think-so too?" And there was the stage when he could run
out crying out: "O now I know! I know!" It is that
conviction which to Paul is faith.

This meaning comes out well in Paul's use of the verb
to believe. And one of the most interesting things in his
letters is the connection of this unshakable belief and conviction with preaching. Preaching is the medium by which
men come to this conviction. He writes to the Corinthians
that it was God's purpose to save them that believe through
the foolishness of preaching (*I Corinthians* 1.21). He speaks
of Cephas and Apollos and himself as ministers by whom ye
believed (*I Corinthians* 3.5). "So we preached," he says to
the Corinthians, "and so ye believed" (*I Corinthians*
15.11). In *I Thessalonians* 1.7 he speaks of all that believe
in Macedonia. In *I Thessalonians* he writes, "If we believe
that Jesus died and rose again . . ." (*I Thessalonians* 4.14),
that is to say, "If we accept the fact of the Resurrection of

Jesus Christ." In *II Thessalonians* 1.10 he writes: "Our testimony was believed," that is to say, it was accepted as true.

To Paul preaching and belief went hand in hand. How could a man be moved to belief and to faith unless he was presented with the christian message? "How then shall they call on him in whom they have not believed? How shall they believe in him of whom they have not heard? And how shall they hear without a preacher?" (*Romans* 10.14).

Here, then, are two great christian facts.

1. Conviction is an essential part of Christianity. Christianity may begin, but cannot ultimately end, with a kind of vague, nebulous emotional response and reaction to the wonder of Jesus Christ. It must go on to try and to test things and to hold fast to that which is good. "The unexamined life," said Plato, "is the life not worth living," and the unexamined faith is the faith not worth having. Where the heart has gone the mind must follow.

2. Preaching is the medium which produces conviction. Preaching is therefore the proclamation of certainties, and the confirmation of belief. Preaching is designed, not to produce questions, but to answer questions; preaching is designed, not to awaken doubts, but to settle and to conquer doubts. The preacher who uses the pulpit to air his own intellectual doubts is doing his people a grave disservice. He will have to state the doubts and the difficulties; but he will have to state them to answer them, not to leave them unsolved. "Tell me of your certainties," said Goethe. "I have doubts enough of my own."

It is often said that the idea of faith as faith in a creed does not occur in the New Testament until as late as the Pastoral Epistles. In a sense that is true, and it is true because the creed of the early Church was quite simply: "Jesus Christ is Lord" (*Philippians* 2.11). But quite often faith stands in the letters of Paul for what we can only call The Christian Religion. Christianity is The Faith. It is Paul's advice to receive him who is weak in the faith, but not to doubtful disputations (*Romans* 14.1). That is to say:

Welcome the man whose Christianity is not yet firmly based, but not to debatable things, which can only shake his faith. In *Galatians* 1.23 he tells them that the Palestinian Christians were bewildered that he was preaching the faith which once he had sought to destroy; that is, that he was preaching the religion which once he had tried to wipe out. In *Colossians* 1.23 he urges his friends to continue in the faith, grounded and settled. In *Colossians* 2.7 he speaks of being stablished in the faith. In *I Corinthians* 16.13 he urges the Corinthians to stand fast in the faith. He writes to the Thessalonians to tell them that he is glad that their faith is growing exceedingly (*II Thessalonians* 1.3). In *II Corinthians* 13.5 he advises his opponents to examine themselves to see if they are in the faith.

In these passages the faith means the christian religion. But the very use of the word is suggestive : Christianity is not allegiance to a creed; it is faith in a person. Christianity is not a system; it is a faith. Jesus' own practice on earth will illuminate this. When he came to men, he did not say to them : " I have a system that I would like you to examine; I have a philosophy I would like you to discuss; I have a theory I would like to lay before you." He said : " Follow me." That is far from saying that the day would not come when the implications, and the whys and wherefores would not need to be thought out and examined until intellectual conviction followed on the heart's response; but it is to say that the moving force of Christianity is in fact this act of personal faith in Jesus Christ.

Faith in the sense of confident hope is a conception which is more characteristic of the writer to the Hebrews than it is of Paul. His great definition of faith was : " Faith is the substance of things hoped for, the evidence of things not seen " (*Hebrews* 11.1). But this idea does occur in Paul. On one occasion at least, Paul comes near to making faith and hope one and the same thing, when he says : " We walk by faith, not by sight " (*II Corinthians* 5.7). Their faith is a sure and certain hope by which they can walk, even when the path is dark. As Donald Hankey had it : " Faith is betting your life there is a God." Faith is the hope which has gone beyond hope and turned to certainty, even when the evidence and the facts seem all against it.

It is true that all these things of which we have been thinking are included in the Pauline conception of faith; but it is also true that, although they are to Paul vital parts of faith, they are not the real centre and soul of faith. We shall come nearer to the Pauline idea of faith, if we go on to see the things which Paul believed could come by faith, and in no other way.

Justification comes by faith. " Therein," he writes, " is the righteousness of God revealed from faith to faith; as it is written, ' The just shall live by faith ' " (*Romans* 1.17). In *Romans* 3.28 he writes : " Therefore we conclude that a man is justified by faith." In *Romans* 5.1 he speaks of the peace with God which comes to those who are justified by faith. In *Galatians* 3.8 he speaks of the scripture foreseeing that God would justify the heathen by faith. The great key passage is in *Galatians* 2.16 : " Knowing that a man is not justified by the works of the law, but by the faith of Jesus Christ, even we have believed in Jesus Christ, that we might be justified by the faith of Christ, and not by the works of the law : for by the works of the law shall no flesh be justified." Let us stop to remember what *justification* means. The Greek word to justify is *dikaioun*. Greek verbs which end in *-oun* never mean to make a person something. They always mean to treat, to reckon, to account a person as something. So when it is said that God justifies us, it does not in the first instance mean that God makes us righteous; it means that God treats us as if we were righteous, even when, in fact, we are sinners. It means that in his amazing and incredible mercy and grace God treats the bad man as if he had been a good man. If we were to receive our deserts, if there happened that which we have every reason to expect would happen, we would stand as criminals before the bar of God's judgment and leave it utterly and completely condemned without defence. But in point of fact the amazing thing is that God accepts us and loves us and welcomes us and receives us, sinners as we are.

The condition which results from that is what Paul calls

righteousness. Righteousness to Paul is not in the first instance moral excellence and rectitude. It is being in a right
relationship with God. If we received our deserts, the only
possible relationship between us and God would be utter
enmity and utter estrangement; but again in this incredible
grace of his, sinners as we are, God has put us in a relationship of loving fellowship with himself. That is what
Paul means when he speaks of the righteousness of God
which is by faith of Jesus Christ (*Romans* 3.22); when he
speaks of righteousness which is of faith (*Romans* 10.6);
when he speaks of the righteousness which is through the
faith of Christ, the righteousness which is of God by faith
(*Philippians* 3.9). In all these cases by righteousness Paul
means that right relationship with God which ought
humanly speaking to have been impossible for sinners, but
which in the mercy of God is made available for us.

How can we say that all this happens by faith? Here we
come to the essence of the matter. We have just been
saying that God treats the bad man as if he were a good
man; that God opens the way to a relationship with himself which we could never have deserved, and which we
could never have achieved. But surely the blazing question
is : How do we know that God is like that? How do we
know that God treats men like that? How can we be certain that these amazingly incredible things are true? The
answer is : Because Jesus told us that God is like that. Our
whole relationship with God is based on unquestioning
faith that what Jesus said about God is true. That is what
justification by faith, righteousness by faith, means. It is
only through faith in Jesus Christ that we can believe these
things.

But another blazing question arises. How could Jesus
know that God is like that? Where did Jesus get his special
knowledge of God? How can we be sure that Jesus was
right about God? The answer is that we are certain that
Jesus was right because we believe that Jesus is so closely
identified with God, if you like to put it so, that Jesus knows
God so well, that we can only call him the Son of God. Our
whole relationship with God is dependent on the faith that

what Jesus said is true, and the faith that Jesus is the Son of God, and therefore not mistaken.

In *Galatians* 3.26 Paul puts this in another way. He says that by faith we become children of God. Left to ourselves we could not conceive of God being anything other than our enemy. On any human grounds we could not conceive of ourselves as receiving anything other than condemnation from God. With such power of thought as we can bring to bear upon this it is incredible that the holiness of God should ever welcome any approach from the sin of man. That is precisely the Old Testament position. Moses heard God say : " No man shall see me and live " (*Exodus* 33.20). When Manoah discovered who his heavenly visitor had been, his terrified cry was : " We shall surely die, because we have seen God " (*Judges* 13.22). Into this terror and estrangement and distance and enmity there comes Christianity with the message that God is eager to welcome men to himself, just as they are. How can anyone believe that? It can only be believed when we take Jesus absolutely and completely at his word; and when we believe that he has the right to speak because he is who he is.

That is what faith means for Paul. We shall go on to develop this still further, but here we are already at the heart of the matter. Faith is complete trust and complete surrender to Jesus Christ. It is the total acceptance of all that he said, of all that he offered, and of all that he is. It is the approach to God in complete confidence that all that Jesus said and taught about God is true, and that we can rest our souls in it.

We will understand even more about what Paul means by faith, if we go on to see the other things which Paul says come by faith. *Romans* 3.22 lays down the great truth about which we have been thinking : " Righteousness is by faith unto all that believe." That is to say, the only way to a right relationship with God is to take Jesus at his word, and to cast ourselves on the mercy of God, believing utterly that what Jesus says about God is true.

But in *Romans* 3.25 Paul introduces another idea. We have propitiation through faith in his blood. What then is propitiation? A propitiation is a sacrifice which restores the lost relationship between God and man. A man commits a sin; that sin causes a breach between him and God. That breach is healed when a sacrifice is brought with a humble and a contrite heart. So what Paul is saying is : It cost the life-blood of Jesus Christ, it cost the Cross, to restore the lost relationship between God and man. Faith is the complete trust that that which Jesus Christ has done in his life and in his death opens for us the way to God.

We may put this in another way, and in a simpler way. It may be that for us the idea of sacrifice is difficult to understand, because, unlike the Jews, we have not been brought up in a sacrificial system. But Paul has another way of putting this which is a much more universal way. In *Romans* 5.2 he speaks of access by faith; in *Ephesians* 3.12 he speaks of access with confidence through faith. As we have already seen, the word for access is *prosagōgē*, which is the technical Greek word for access to the presence of a king. Obviously ordinary people do not have access to the presence of an earthly king; an earthly monarch is fenced around with guards and courtiers and palace officials. In the ancient world there was actually an official called the *prosagōgeus*, whose function it was to ward off the undesirable and to introduce the acceptable into the presence of the king. Quite clearly no one would ever dream that sinning men should have access to the presence of the holiness of God; anyone would assume that the sinner is shut out from the presence of God. But the wonder of Christianity is that Jesus Christ came to tell us of the God whose heart and whose door are wide open to the sinner. Once again, apart from Jesus Christ we could never have believed that God is like that; we could never have guessed that God is like that. We can only approach God at all because we believe that God is as Jesus Christ told us that he is. That for Paul is access by faith.

But there is still another connection which is very close to the heart of the thought of Paul. In *Ephesians* 2.8 he writes : " By grace are ye saved through faith." This is a highly compressed saying. We shall later on in our studies have to think much more fully of what Paul means by grace; at the moment we note this. In the Pauline idea of grace there are invariably two elements. Grace is something which is very lovely, and grace is something which is entirely free.

It is the second of these ideas which is always dominant in Paul's thought. Grace is something which we could never deserve, which we could never have earned, something which is given generously and freely for the accepting. Here is the very essence of Pauline religion. The Jew would have said : You must earn the favour of God; you must keep the Law, you must live a life entirely obedient to the Law's commands; and then you will earn and receive the favour of God. The whole duty of a Jew was to earn God's favour. Paul would have said—and he said so because he had tried it—that it is utterly impossible for any man ever to earn the favour of God, that man's imperfection can never satisfy God's perfection, that in relation to God the best man in the world, and the best man who can ever be, is always in default. What then is the consequence? The consequence is that what we cannot earn, we must freely accept and trustingly take. We cannot earn God's love; God's love is offered to us freely and for nothing. That is what grace means.

But again the salient question arises—How can I know that? How can I possibly believe that? How can I believe that God's love is not to be earned, but to be freely and wonderingly accepted? The answer is the same again—apart from Jesus Christ we could never have known that. It is because we believe that Jesus told us the truth about God that we believe in the grace of God.

There is still one other way by which Paul comes at this. He says first of all that Jesus is the power of God unto salvation to everyone that believes (*Romans* 1.16). That means that apart from Jesus Christ, we would be strangers, enemies, criminals in the sight of God. When we accept all that Jesus Christ says as true, then there comes into life the power which makes us friends with God again. Paul has one other way of putting this, and it is the greatest way of all. In *Ephesians* 3.17 it is his hope and prayer that Christ may dwell in our hearts through faith. His prayer is that we will never at any time doubt what he says, that we will never at any time question his offer, that we will absolutely and without argument or doubt take his word about God, and so enter into this new relationship of fellowship with God.

With all this in our minds, let us turn to the man who was Paul's perfect illustration of faith. Paul knew quite well that very few people can grasp abstract truths and abstract ideas; he was a wise teacher and he knew that nearly everyone thinks in pictures and that, if we want to present a person with an idea, that idea must become vivid and concrete and dramatic in a picture. So Paul turns the word faith into flesh; he turns the idea of faith into a person, and that person is Abraham. It is in *Romans* 4 and *Galatians* 3 that this idea is most fully worked out. Abraham was justified; that is to say, Abraham was in a right relationship with God. How did Abraham arrive at that right relationship? It was certainly not by keeping the Law, for the simple reason that the Law was not given until four hundred years after Abraham was dead. It was certainly not through circumcision because Abraham was in his right relationship with God years before he was circumcised. The promise and the blessing and the right relationship came to Abraham quite independently of the Law and of circumcision.

Wherein then lay Abraham's faith? Put at its very briefest—Abraham went out not knowing whither he went. Put in another way—Abraham took God absolutely and completely at his word. Let us put it in still another way—Abraham's faith was compounded of perfect trust and absolute obedience. Abraham took God at his word when God promised and when God commanded, and that is faith.

On any reasonable and logical view of the matter there can be nothing but distance between God and man. Measuring the matter by human standards, man could expect nothing but judgment and nothing but condemnation from God. But the very essence of Christianity is that the relationship between man and God is not distance, but fellowship; and the attitude of God to man is not condemnation, but love.

But we ought to remind ourselves again and again and again that we could never have known that, we could never have guessed that, we could never even in our wildest dreams have hoped for that, apart from Jesus Christ. Everything we know of the mercy and the love of God goes straight back to Jesus Christ. That is what all Christianity is founded on, faith in Jesus Christ. We would never possess even the beginnings of the religion we possess unless we took Jesus Christ at his word when he tells us the good news about God. And it is that taking of Jesus at his word which is faith. Let us now see if we can develop that a little further.

The first element in faith is what we can only call receptivity. In *Romans* 10.17 Paul uses a very significant phrase when he speaks of " faith which comes by hearing ". An offer has first to be heard and then to be received. A man can confront the message of Jesus Christ either with a blank and blunt refusal to listen to it at all, or else with a shut and closed mind which refuses to take it in. In both cases faith is impossible. Faith begins with the consent to listen to Jesus Christ with an open mind. In any event, apart altogether from the religious side of the matter, no honest and honourable man condemns anyone without giving him a hearing. Faith begins with giving the message of Jesus Christ a hearing—and an honest man is bound to do that.

The second element in faith is what we might call the assent of the mind. There can be no faith without the belief that God exists; there can be no faith without the belief that Jesus Christ did come to this earth and that he was who he was.

Every now and again we are confronted with an attack on Christianity which seeks to prove that Jesus never

existed, that he is in fact nothing but a myth or a legend.
That attack must always collapse on one basic fact. Suppose we assess the evidence for the Battle of Hastings,
wherein does the strength of that evidence lie? In the last
analysis it does not lie in the history books and the
chronicles and the annals. It lies in the state of this
country today. The Norman arches of the most ancient
cathedrals and churches, the government and the administration of this country, the racial characteristics of the
people, the whole way of life which we have inherited and
which we live, apart altogether from anything that chronicles and stories and history books may say, demonstrate the
truth of the fact that the Normans did conquer this country;
and the evidence for the historical existence of Jesus Christ
lies not in the gospels or in any history book; it lies in the
state of this world today.

We have simply to compare the world before and the
world after Christ. Whence came that new code of sexual
purity? Whence came that new passion for social justice?
Whence came that new respect for women, that new love
of children, that new care for the weak and the sick and
the deformed and the aged and the poor? There was one
world before and another world after the emergence of
Jesus Christ in history. The evidence for the existence of
Jesus Christ lies in life itself.

But further, not only must we believe that Jesus did live
and die, and rise again, we must also believe that he is the
person he claimed to be. We need not express that in any
one way, but we must assent to the uniqueness of Jesus
Christ; we must assent to his unique right to speak of and
to speak for God. Jesus is not one voice among many
speaking about God; he is not even the greatest of the voices
who spoke about God; he is in a unique sense the voice of
God.

Faith then begins with receptivity; it goes on to an
assent of the mind to the basic facts. But faith goes far
beyond that. We can put this third step this way—faith is
not only assent to the facts; faith is still more assent to the

significance of the facts. Or may we put that in another way—faith is not merely the assent of the mind to Jesus Christ; it is the assent of the whole man to Jesus Christ.

Intellectual assent by itself is not nearly enough. James put this matter most bluntly : " Thou believest that there is one God; thou doest well : the devils also believe, and tremble " (*James* 2.19). Let us see how Paul himself puts it : " If thou shalt confess with thy mouth the Lord Jesus and shall believe in thine heart that God hath raised him from the dead, thou shalt be saved" (*Romans* 10.9). This is a belief, a faith, which resides, not only in the mind, but in the heart.

Let us take the simplest of simple illustrations of the two kinds of belief. I believe that the square on the hypotenuse of a right-angled triangle equals the sum of the squares on the other two sides. I am intellectually convinced of that—but it makes no difference to me. But—I believe that six and six make twelve, and I will therefore resolutely refuse to pay one shilling and two pence for two sixpenny bars of chocolate. The one kind of belief was quite outside my active life; the other kind of belief dominates my active life. In the one case I assent to the facts, but that is all that there is to it; in the other case, I assent to the significance of the facts, and the significance of the facts permeates my every action. That is something like what Paul means when he speaks about believing with the heart. Faith is not simply receptivity of the facts; it is not simply assent to the facts; it is assent to the significance of the facts for life.

But there is one other saying of Paul which must be woven into this pattern. In *Galatians* 5.6 Paul speaks of faith which works, which is set in motion, through love. Here we are getting very near to the heart of things. This final kind of faith is set in motion through love. It is not possible to make a hard and fast, cut and dried, analysis of human thoughts and motives; but in christian faith at its fullest and best there are three steps.

1. A man is confronted with the christian message, either through the word of a preacher, or through the study of God's book. He comes to the decision that he must believe

what Jesus tells him about God; and that he must believe Jesus' own claims. He has made his first act of assent.

2. He is then confronted with what it cost Jesus to bring this message of the love of God, and thus to open the way to God for men. It cost Jesus every sorrow of body, mind and heart which can come to the life of any man. It cost him the hatred of the orthodox churchmen of his day; it cost him the breach with his own nearest and dearest; it cost him the disloyalty of his closest friends; it cost him the scourging, the crown of thorns, the Cross and death. In view of all that a man is bound to say : I am bound to love him who made such a sacrifice for me; such love demands my love. In simple gratitude I cannot do anything else but love this Christ. Faith is now energised by love. First there came the assent; then there came the realisation of what it meant even to make the facts known; and assent kindles into love and passionate devotion.

3. Then there comes the third step which sets the coping-stone on faith, and without which faith is incomplete. A man receives the facts and assents to them; he sees what the facts cost and his love runs out to Jesus Christ. Then he is bound to go on to say : Because I must answer love with love, I will make a complete self-surrender and a complete submission to this Jesus Christ.

Any tremendous gift involves tremendous obligations. No man can in honour take everything and give nothing back. And the coping-stone of faith is in fact obedience. It is the acceptance not only of the offer of grace, but of the obligation of grace.

So now we have complete the three elements in faith. Faith is receptivity; faith comes from hearing the message of Jesus Christ. Either to refuse to listen or to listen with a shut mind makes faith impossible. Faith goes on to assent that this message is true; that God is as Jesus proclaims him to be, and that Jesus has the right to make that proclamation because he stands in a unique relationship to the God of whom he speaks. Faith passes from assent into the realisation of the wondrous love which bore the sacrifice that the proclamation of these facts involved, and faith surrenders in perfect trust and perfect submission and perfect obedience to Jesus Christ. Faith is the total assent of a man's total being to Jesus Christ.

We may sum it up in this way : Faith is the response of trust of a man's total personality to the love of God as shown to us in the life and death of Jesus Christ.

XIII

THE ESSENTIAL GRACE

James Moffatt in his book *Grace in the New Testament* has succinctly laid it down that the very essence and centre of Pauline faith and religion can be summed up in one brief sentence : " All is of grace, and grace is for all." For Paul grace is the essential grace.

We must begin by noting two general facts about grace. These two facts are not exclusively Pauline; they belong to the very nature of the idea of grace. We shall have to return to them more fully, but at the moment we state them briefly.

First, grace is in essence a lovely thing. The Greek word for grace is *charis,* and *charis* can mean *physical beauty,* everything that is contained in the word *charm.* Grace always moves in the realm of winsomeness, of loveliness, of attractiveness, of beauty and of charm. The word has in it all the beauty of holiness. There are certain christian terms which inevitably have in them an idea and an atmosphere of sternness and of severity. But grace, in the christian sense, is a thing of such surpassing beauty that the heart bows down in wondering adoration before it. There is an old hymn which has the line : " Grace 'tis a charming sound," and there is a world of truth there.

Second, grace had always in it the idea of a gift, which is completely free and entirely undeserved. The ideas of grace and merit are mutually exclusive and completely contradictory. No one can earn grace; it can only be humbly, gratefully and adoringly received. Grace is something which is given, as we say, *gratis*. The fundamental idea of grace is a gift, given out of the sheer generosity of the giver's heart, a gift which the receiver could never have earned and could never have deserved by any efforts of his own.

When Paul laid such stress on grace, he set out on a road of thought which was quite strange to the orthodox Jewish teaching of his day. It is true that in its highest and most devotional moments Jewish religion did rest in the mercy of God and in nothing else. From the daily prayer book of the Jews there comes the prayer which every Jew still knows : " Sovereign of the worlds, not because of our righteous deeds do we present our supplications before thee, but because of thine abundant mercies." On this prayer Abrahams comments : " Rewards and punishments were meted out in some sort of accordance with a man's righteousness and sin, yet nothing that a man with his small powers and finite opportunities can do constitutes a claim on the favour of the Almighty and the Infinite. In the final resort, all that a man receives from the divine hand is an act of grace." There speaks the highest and most devoted thought of Judaism; but that is not representative of the teaching of the orthodox Rabbis in the days of Paul.

Much more representative of orthodox Judaism is the passage in the *Sayings of the Fathers* (3.22ff) : " The world is ruled by goodness, yet everything is according to the amount of work." That saying is closely followed by a kind of parable or allegory : Everything is given on pledge (i.e. on pledge of repayment) and the net (i.e. of destiny) is spread all over the living. The shop is opened and the shopman (or money-lender) gives credit; the account-book is opened and the hand writes; everyone who desires to borrow comes and borrows; but the collectors (i.e. the angels) go round continually every day and exact payment from a man, whether he knows it or not (i.e. whether or not he is aware that calamity and sorrow and sickness are the result and the payment of the debt); and they (the collectors) have that on which they rely. And the judgment is a judgment of truth (i.e. accurate and fair); men have to pay what they owe but no more.

That is the accounting and the legalistic idea of religion. It looks on the relationship between God and man as a relationship of debit and of credit; it looks on religion as something which either earns so much credit, or incurs so much debt.

In the *Mishnah* there is the sentence : " It was because the holy One wished to give Israel an opportunity to acquire merit that he gave them so much *Torah* (Law) and so many commandments." The Law was designed to enable a man to amass and to acquire credit in the sight of God. Moffatt quotes Marmorstein as summing the matter up : everything depends on the assumption that " Man has got the ability to acquire merits before the heavenly Father ". However weak and frail man may be, physically and morally, he is in a position to gather merits in the eyes of God.

Nothing could be more diametrically opposed to the conception of Paul. To Paul the essential idea of all religion is grace, and grace means that no man can ever acquire anything in the sight of God; that all that man can do is wonderingly to accept that which God freely and generously gives.

We may see the position that grace held in the mind of Paul, when we see that every single letter that Paul ever wrote begins and ends with grace. It is worth while to list Paul's beginnings and endings :—

Romans 1.7. To all that be in Rome, beloved of God, called to be saints : Grace to you and peace from God our Father, and the Lord Jesus Christ.

Romans 16.24. The grace of our Lord Jesus Christ be with you all.

I Corinthians 1.2, 3. Unto the Church of God which is at Corinth . . . grace be unto you, and peace, from God our Father, and from the Lord Jesus Christ.

I Corinthians 16.23. The grace of our Lord Jesus Christ be with you.

II Corinthians 1.1, 2. Paul, an apostle of Jesus Christ by the will of God . . . unto the Church of God which is at Corinth . . . Grace be to you and peace from the Lord Jesus Christ.

II Corinthians 13.14. The grace of the Lord Jesus Christ, and the love of God, and the communion of the Holy Ghost, be with you all.

Galatians 1.1-3. Paul, an apostle . . . unto the churches of Galatia, grace be to you and peace from God the Father, and from our Lord Jesus Christ.

Galatians 6.18. Brethren, the grace of our Lord Jesus Christ be with your spirit.

Ephesians 1.1. Paul, an apostle of Jesus Christ . . . to the saints which are at Ephesus, and to the faithful in Christ Jesus, grace be to you and peace, from God our Father, and from the Lord Jesus Christ.

Ephesians 6.24. Grace be with all them that love our Lord Jesus Christ in sincerity.

Philippians 1.1. Paul and Timothy . . . to all the saints in Christ Jesus which are at Philippi . . . grace be unto you, and peace from God our Father, and from the Lord Jesus Christ.

Philippians 4.23. The grace of our Lord Jesus Christ be with you all.

Colossians 1.1, 2. Paul an apostle of Jesus Christ . . . to the saints and faithful brethren in Christ which are at Colosse; grace be unto you and peace from God our Father and the Lord Jesus Christ.

Colossians 4.18. The salutation by the hand of me Paul. Remember my bonds. Grace be with you.

I Thessalonians 1.1. Paul . . . unto the Church of the Thessalonians . . . grace be unto you and peace from God our Father, and the Lord Jesus Christ.

I Thessalonians 5.28. The grace of our Lord Jesus Christ be with you.

II Thessalonians 1.1, 2. Paul . . . unto the Church of the Thessalonians . . . grace unto you, and peace from God our Father, and the Lord Jesus Christ.

II Thessalonians 3.18. The grace of our Lord Jesus Christ be with you all.

Philemon 3. Paul, a prisoner of Jesus Christ . . . unto Philemon . . . grace to you and peace, from God our Father and the Lord Jesus Christ.

Philemon 25. The grace of the Lord Jesus Christ be with your spirit.

Every letter Paul wrote begins by striking the note of grace and ends by leaving the sound of grace ringing in men's ears.

When Paul thought and wrote like this, he was thinking and writing out of the depths and heights of his own religious experience. He knew what he had been, and he knew what he was—and there was no possible explanation of the change other than the grace of God. He knew of the work that once he had been doing, and he knew of the work which now had been given him to do; he knew how the persecutor had become the apostle; and only grace could explain that transformation. He knew what the heathen world was like, and he knew what a man could become in Christ, and the only possible explanation of that recreation was the grace of God. To Paul grace was central because he could never forget what grace had done for him, and daily he was seeing what grace could do for all men who would receive it.

When we read Paul's letters, we see, even on the most cursory reading, that Paul can speak without distinction of the grace of God and of the grace of Jesus Christ. In *1 Corinthians* 1.4 he writes of "the grace of God which is given you by Jesus Christ." In *Galatians* 2.21 he says: "I do not frustrate the grace of God." But in *1 Corinthians* 16.23 he speaks of the grace of our Lord Jesus Christ, as he does in *Philippians* 4.23; *Galatians* 6.18; *Romans* 16.24. And in all his opening addresses in his letters he speaks of the grace of God our Father and of the Lord Jesus Christ. Here again we are reminded of two great Pauline facts which we have often seen before.

First, behind everything is the initiative of God. The grace is God's grace; the offering love is the love of God; the initiative is the divine initiative. From this point of view the passage in *1 Corinthians* 1.4 is very illuminating; it speaks of the grace of God which is given to you *en Christō Iesou,* which can equally well mean *by Jesus Christ* or *in*

Jesus Christ. It was God's grace which was mediated to men by Jesus Christ; or, if we care to put it more vividly, but just as accurately, Jesus Christ is the incarnate Grace of God. Jesus is not only the channel or the expression of God's grace to men, great as that would be : he *is* God's grace to men.

Second, the fact that Paul begins his letters with the message of grace from God the Father and from the Lord Jesus Christ means that the mind of Jesus and the mind of God are one and the same; and the attitude of God and the attitude of Jesus to men are identical. Looking at this, as we might say, from the point of view of Jesus, we may say that Jesus did not come to this world by compulsion or by coercion, not even as one under orders, but because in him there was the heart of God which is the heart of grace and love. Looking at this, as we might say, from the point of view of God, we may say that in no way did the coming of Jesus change or alter the attitude of God to men, in no way did anything that Jesus did change the wrath of God into the love of God, for the grace that is in Jesus is the grace of God. The love which Jesus demonstrated is the love of God. Grace is the grace of God and of the Lord Jesus Christ.

Let us now seek to bring to light the main Pauline ideas behind the conception of grace.

We must begin with that most basic of all ideas, an idea which we have already mentioned. The basic idea behind the conception of grace is the undeserved generosity of God. The idea of grace is the idea of God's forgiveness of man as a free gift, which man could never have deserved or earned, and which is given in the sheer generosity of God. In *I Corinthians* 1.4 Paul speaks of "the grace of God which is given to you". In *Ephesians* 3.7 he speaks of the gift of the grace of God. In *II Corinthians* 6.1 he pleads with the Corinthians not to receive the grace of God in vain. Grace is something which can only be received. In *II Corinthians* 8.1 he speaks of the grace bestowed upon the Churches in Macedonia. Grace is something which is bestowed, not earned. In *II Corinthians* 8.9 the grace of

Jesus is demonstrated by the fact that he who was rich for our sakes became poor. Grace is this undeserved sacrifice of the love of God; it is the generosity of God for us and to us. In *Romans* 4.4 grace and debt are contrasted. Payment, contract, debt are something which a man earns and incurs, and to which he has a right; grace is something unearned and undeserved. In *Romans* 11.6 grace and works are contrasted. If works determine the relationship between God and man, then grace is no longer grace. The idea of merit and the idea of grace contradict each other. In *Ephesians* 1.6 it is said that it is by grace that we are accepted in the beloved. Our acceptance is not something merited; it is something given. In *Ephesians* 2.5-9 Paul lays it down with all the emphasis at his command that it is by grace that we are saved. Man's salvation is due neither to any merit nor to any effort of his own, but is dependent solely on the sheer mercy and love of God. Even the faintest idea of achievement is ruled out.

All through his letters Paul is entranced and engrossed with the conviction that grace is the gift of the generosity of God, which man can neither earn nor achieve, but which he can only take and receive.

We must further note that for Paul there is a certain inexhaustible abundance in the grace of God. In *II Corinthians* 9.14 he speaks of the exceeding grace of God; in *II Corinthians* 9.8 he tells the Corinthians that God is able to make all grace abound to them. In *Romans* 5.20 there is the triumphant claim that where sin abounded grace did much more abound. In *Ephesians* 1.7 Paul speaks of the riches of his grace; and in *Ephesians* 2.7 of the exceeding riches of his grace.

Grace is not a thing of narrow limitations, it is not a thing measured out in painstakingly accurate quantities with just enough and no more, as an ingredient might be in a recipe for some concoction; in grace there is a certain infinity; a certain complete adequacy; a certain inexhaustibility and illimitableness. No demand that can ever be made on it can exhaust it or strain its capacity and its power.

There is a corollary to this. As Moffatt put it in a vivid

phrase : "Grace needs no supplement." It is by grace and grace alone that men are saved : nothing else is needful; in fact the introduction of anything else destroys the whole principle of salvation. This is the principle on which Paul insists in two of his greatest epistles.

It is the argument which is at the basis of *Romans*. The idea that Paul is there combatting is the idea which willingly accepts the fact that there is such a thing as grace, but holds that the operation of grace must be buttressed and helped by the performance of works designed to gain merit. In that telegraphic verse in *Romans* 11.6 Paul lays it down. "And if by grace, then it is no more of works; otherwise grace is no more grace. But if it be of works, then is it no more grace; otherwise work is no more work." To Paul grace and works are mutually exclusive principles. If salvation has anything to do with works, then it is not of grace; it is of merit. If salvation be a thing of pure grace, then works do not enter into the matter, for merit cannot enter into the matter. We cannot set out to save ourselves by works, and then drag in the principle of grace; we cannot accept the principle that we are saved by grace, and then drag in works. The two exclude each other. If salvation is by works, then there is no such thing as grace; and if grace is grace, it needs no supplement, but is all sufficient. The same argument recurs in *Galatians*. The Galatians did not deny the existence of grace. Their position was : Grace there is; but the work of grace has to be buttressed by the acceptance of circumcision and the acceptance of the Law. To put it bluntly, they said : A man cannot be saved by grace alone; to God's grace he must add his own circumcision and his own performance of the works of the Law. To God's grace he must add his own meritwinning performance.

In face of this way of thinking Paul flings his great challenge : " I do not frustrate the grace of God; for, if righteousness come by the Law, then Christ is dead in vain " (*Galatians* 2.21). If a man can be saved by his own efforts, if by meticulous performance of the works of the Law a man can establish the right relationship between himself and God, then the death of Christ was a colossal mistake, and his sacrifice was a completely unnecessary sacrifice.

Paul's whole position was : Accept the position that works are efficacious for the obtaining of salvation, and you have accepted the position that man by his unaided efforts can acquire merit in the sight of God; and simply to state that possibility is to obliterate the fact and the need of grace. But accept the position that all is of grace, that all is the generous gift of God, and nothing further is needed. To bring in anything further is to deny the full sufficiency and the full adequacy of grace.

Once again it is from personal experience that Paul is speaking. For Paul righteousness consists in a right relationship with God; to put it very simply, righteousness is friendship with God. All his life Paul strove for that friendship. He tried to attain to it by a meticulous performance of the works of the Law, for he could claim that in his performance of the demands of the Law he was blameless (*Philippians* 3.6). And the only result of all this was that he was as far, and farther, away from God. Then in the face of the Cross he determined to fling himself quite simply on the mercy of God; and the peace of the right relationship with God came to him in a flash. God's grace had done what all his own works were powerless to do. Paul had made the great discovery that divine grace needs no human additions to be effective for salvation. For Paul that was the beginning of the Christian way, although as we shall yet see it was not the end.

Paul was convinced that we are saved by grace; but Paul would have gone further than that. Paul insisted that we are not only saved by grace, but that we are also called by grace. It is not only the final work that is the work of grace; the first movings, the first stirrings, the first faint desirings in a man's heart, are also the work of grace. The grace of God does not only save a man; the grace of God also shows a man his need to be saved and puts into his heart the desire for salvation. *Galatians* 1.6 speaks of the Galatians as being called into the grace of Christ. *Romans* 11.5 speaks of the election of grace. Our realisation that we are sinners, our penitence and our contrition are also the work of grace.

Here we have something which is of great importance. We have seen how Paul, especially in the later epistles, thinks in terms of the pre-existent Christ. We have also seen that Jesus Christ may be looked on as the embodiment and essence of the grace of God. Now if Jesus Christ was pre-existent and eternal, it means that God's grace is eternal. God's grace is not a kind of emergency measure which was introduced when a world founded on merit had collapsed; God's grace was not something which came in when the Law had been found to be impossible. The gracious purpose of God is the eternal purpose of God. God's grace was there before all time. God is the God of grace, yesterday, today and for ever.

All through his letters Paul makes it clear that he was convinced that not only his eternal salvation, but his whole personal life, his place and task in the world and in God's scheme of things were bound up with grace. This grace was working on him before he could ever have any conception that it was working.

It was that grace which separated him from his mother's womb and called him (*Galatians* 1.15). In *II Corinthians* 1.1 he says that he is an apostle by the will of God. These two sayings are very suggestive for they say the same thing in different ways. The first says that it was God's grace which made Paul an apostle; the second says that it was God's will which made Paul an apostle. That is to say, these two sayings equate God's grace and God's will. In other words, the grace of God is the will of God in action on the lives of men.

It is the grace of God which gave Paul the task of preaching among the Gentiles the unsearchable riches of Christ (*Ephesians* 3.8). It is the grace of God which enabled Paul like a wise master-builder to lay the foundations of the faith of the Corinthians (*I Corinthians* 3.10). It is by the grace of God that he has his talk and conversation in the world (*II Corinthians* 1.12). It was the evident fact that the grace of God had been given to him in relation to his task among the Gentiles which persuaded the leaders of the Church to accept him and, as it were, to ratify his special commission (*Galatians* 2.9). When Paul speaks, it is through the grace of God that he does speak. " I say," he writes to the Romans, " through the grace given unto me to every man that is among you not to think of himself more highly than he ought to think " (*Romans* 12.3). To sum it up, Paul is what he is by grace and nothing else. " By the grace of God I am what I am : and his grace which was bestowed upon me was not in vain; but I laboured more abundantly than they all; yet not I, but the grace of God which was with me " (*I Corinthians* 15.10).

Here again we have one of these illuminating parallels. This passage from *I Corinthians* is bound to turn our thoughts to the companion passage in *Galatians* 2.20 : " I live; yet not I, but Christ liveth in me." In the one passage it is the grace of God which is in Paul; in the other passage it is Christ who is in him. The principle of Paul's life is grace; and the principle of Paul's life is Christ. Paul equates grace and Christ; both mean the same. Grace is Christ, and Christ is grace.

But it is not to be thought that Paul connected grace with only the great events and the great experiences of life. To Paul grace is the power which enables men to meet with gallantry and with adequacy the demands, the responsibilities, and the tasks of this life.

In *II Thessalonians* 2.15-17 Paul is encouraging the Thessalonians to stand fast in the midst of the persecution and hardship which the christian life necessarily involves; and the ground of his request is that God " has given us everlasting consolation and good hope through grace ". It was grace alone which could take them through the threatening stretches of this life.

Still more, it was grace which enabled Paul to carry on the routine business of life when he was up against it. He tells of the thorn in his flesh, and of his prayers that it should be taken away from him. He tells that that release was not to be; but the answer came : " My grace is sufficient for you " (*II Corinthians* 12.9). It was by that grace he lived every day; and in that grace he met the routine tasks of every day.

Still further, it is grace that is responsible for any nobility that there is in life. In *II Corinthians* 1.12 Paul attributes his sincerity to the grace of God. In *II Corinthians* 8.7 he attributes the liberality and the generosity of his converts to grace. In *Galatians* 5.22, 23 the great qualities of the christian life are called the fruit of the Spirit. The work of grace and the work of the Spirit are the same. The Spirit is the bringer of grace; and grace is the power of the Spirit on the lives of men.

Grace is that power of God which clothes a man with day-to-day fortitude and strength. Grace is that power of God which adorns a man's life with lovely things. Grace is a man's day-to-day defence and inspiration. Grace is not only the glory of the mountain top; it is the source of strength for the ordinary road of the everyday.

There remains one side of the question still to be considered, and it can only be called the obligation of grace. Twice Paul uses a suggestive phrase, once of himself and once of his converts. In *I Corinthians* 15.10 he says that the grace of God was not bestowed upon him in vain. In *II Corinthians* 6.1 he beseeches his converts not to receive the grace of God in vain. In the latter cases the phrase is *eis kenon,* literally *for emptiness.*

Here is the other side of the question. It is here that the balance is preserved and that works come in. We can say that works have nothing to do with salvation; but we dare not say that works have nothing to do with the christian life. Paul was far too good a Jew ever to say that, for Judaism was supremely an ethical religion. Christianity was a religion which issued in a certain way of life. Was not its first title The Way?

A man is saved by grace. What is the result of that? The result is that it lays upon a man the tremendous obligation to spend his life showing that that grace was not expended on him in vain. In grace there has reached out to him the love of God; he must therefore be filled with the unutterable longing and the burning desire to show himself, by the help of that grace, worthy of that grace. This is out of the sphere of law altogether; this is no legal obligation; it is not a case of doing good or being good, because the opposite would entail some legal penalty and punishment; it is a case of doing good and being good, because a man cannot bear to disappoint the love which has loved him so.

Here is what is at the back of *Romans* 6. At the back of that chapter there is an argument. The misguided ones say to Paul : " You believe that God's grace is the biggest thing in the world?" " Yes," answers Paul. " You believe that God's grace is wide enough to forgive any sin?" " Yes." Then the misguided ones go on to argue : " If that be so, let us go on sinning to our heart's content. God will forgive. Nay, more, the more we sin, the more chances this wonderful grace of God will receive to abound. Let us continue in sin that grace may get more chances to abound."

The whole essence of that argument is that it is a legal argument. Basically it says that we can go on sinning, because sin will not be punished, and grace will find a way of escape. But Paul's whole position is the lover's position : he cannot make the grace which loved him so of no effect; he must spend all life in one great endeavour to show how much he loves the God who loved him so much. That is the obligation of grace. That is where works come in.

Here is the balance we need. We can never be saved by works; but, if our salvation does not issue in works, it is not salvation. It is not first works, and then salvation. It is first salvation, and then works. We do not become saved by keeping the Law; we can only keep the Law because we are saved. All is of love, and a man cannot accept God's grace, and then go on to break the heart of the God who loved him so much.

XIV

PAUL'S THINKING ABOUT THE HOLY SPIRIT

When Jesus left this world in the body, it was his promise that he would send the Holy Spirit to his people (*John* 14.16, 17, 26; 16.7, 13). It is therefore clear that the doctrine of the Holy Spirit is one of the most important doctrines in the christian faith. It is quite true that the Holy Spirit is some one to be experienced, and not some thing to be talked and argued about. Nevertheless it will be salutary for us to see the greatness of Paul's thinking about the Spirit.

We must begin by noting that here, as everywhere else, Paul leads all things straight back to God. Here as everywhere his uncompromising monotheism and his conviction of the fundamental supremacy of God dominate all his thinking.

Paul is certain that the Holy Spirit is the gift of God. In *I Thessalonians* 4.8 he speaks of God who has also given unto us his Holy Spirit. The Holy Spirit, as Paul sees the matter, comes to men through the announcement of the christian gospel which produces faith in men's hearts. We may put two of Paul's sayings together. In *Romans* 10.17 Paul says that faith comes by hearing, and hearing by the word of God. In *Galatians* 3.2, 5 he speaks of receiving the Spirit by the hearing of faith. The Spirit is received by men as a consequence of their hearing and accepting in faith the gospel which is preached to them. The Holy Spirit is God's gift to men, and comes to men when men react in faith to the message of good news sent by God.

Here, right at the beginning, we are face to face with an essential fact. The coming of the Holy Spirit into a man's life is not something which a man can win or achieve or gain by his own efforts; it is something which a man must accept and receive in faith. It is one of the great and simple facts of the christian life that we cannot receive the Spirit of God unless we are prepared to wait patiently and prayerfully and expectantly for the coming of the Spirit.

More than once Paul uses a curious and a vivid phrase about the Holy Spirit. In *II Corinthians* 1.22 he speaks of God who has given us the *earnest* of the Spirit. In *II Corinthians* 5.5 he speaks of God giving us the *earnest* of the Spirit. In *Ephesians* 1.14 he speaks of the Spirit who is the *earnest* of our inheritance.

The word which the Authorized Version translates *earnest* is the Greek word *arrabōn*. This is a word which very frequently appears in contracts and agreements. Amongst the papyri many of these contracts still exist, and this word occurs in them. A woman sells a cow and she receives one thousand *drachmae* as an *arrabōn* that in due time the remainder of the purchase price will be paid. A troop of castanet dancing-girls are engaged for a village festival; they are paid so many *drachmae* in advance as an *arrabōn*, with a proviso that this sum will be taken into account when the final payment is made, after the performance has been duly given. An *arrabōn* was an advance payment; it was a first instalment; it was a part-payment which was a pledge and a guarantee that in due time the full payment would be made.

Here we have a great thought. The gift of the Holy Spirit is the first instalment of that perfect blessedness which God has prepared for those who love him. The life which is lived in the Spirit is a foretaste and a guarantee of the life of heaven itself.

Very often Paul uses the conception of the Spirit in a very special way. All through his writings there runs a contrast between flesh and spirit. Often the two words occur in juxtaposition, the one expressing the opposite of the other. In *Galatians* 3.3 Paul protests that those who began in the Spirit now think that they can be made perfect in the flesh. In *Galatians* 5.16ff he contrasts walking in the Spirit with fulfilling the lusts of the flesh, and he contrasts the fruit of the Spirit, and the fruit of the flesh. In *Galatians*

6.8 he contrasts those who sow to the flesh, and thereby reap corruption, and those who sow to the Spirit, and thereby reap life everlasting. *Romans* 8 is full of this contrast. In *Romans* 8.5 he contrasts those who are after the flesh and who mind the things of the flesh, and those who are after the Spirit and who mind the things of the Spirit. In *Romans* 8.9 he insists that his converts are no longer in the flesh but are in the Spirit. More than once (e.g. *Romans* 8.1) he urges his converts to walk, not after the flesh, but after the Spirit. For Paul the Spirit stood for all God's goodness and God's power and God's way of things as contrasted with the natural evil and the natural propensity to sin of the man without Christ.

In another vivid phrase Paul speaks of the possession of the Spirit as being the *sign* and *seal* that a man belongs to God. In *II Corinthians* 1.22 he speaks of God who has *sealed* us, and given us the *earnest* of the Spirit. In *Ephesians* 1.13 he says that his hearers are *sealed* with the Spirit who had been promised. In *Ephesians* 4.30 he urges them not to grieve the Holy Spirit with whom they are *sealed* against the day of redemption.

Just as in the case of the word *arrabōn*, there lies behind this also a trading and commercial and business practice. There were two cases in which a seal was specially significant and important in the ancient world. When a man sealed a document or a will he guaranteed by affixing his seal that it was his, and that he was prepared to stand by the contents and the conditions of it. Further, very frequently goods were sealed. A sack or a package might be closed with a seal placed over the knot in the cord or rope which closed it. The seal was the sender's guarantee that the goods really came from him, and that they were of the standard which he had undertaken to deliver.

The gift of the Spirit is God's seal upon man, guaranteeing the fact that that man belongs to him. When we see a man living with the peace and the power and the joy and the serenity and the wisdom which only the Spirit can bring, that is unanswerable proof that that man belongs to God, and is God's man.

Before ever Christianity came into this world, the Jews had their beliefs about the Spirit of God. The Jews had two basic beliefs about Spirit. They believed that the Spirit was the person who brought and revealed God's truth to men; and they believed that the Spirit was the person who enabled men to recognise the truth, and to understand it, when it came to them.

Again and again Jesus had called the Spirit whom he promised the Spirit of truth. He had said that the Spirit would teach men all things; that the Spirit would bring all things to their remembrance; that the Spirit would guide them into all truth (*John* 14.17, 26; 15.26; 16.13). It was then very natural that Paul should look on the Spirit as the revealer of God's truth to men, as God's agent in revelation.

In *Ephesians* 3.3-5 he speaks of the revelation of that eternal mystery of God which is now revealed by the Holy Spirit to the prophets and to the apostles. In *I Corinthians* 2.11 he insists that, just as only a man's spirit knows the things that are in the man, so only the Spirit of God knows the things of God. He claims that the things which he himself teaches are not the product of man-made or man-discovered wisdom, but the result of the revelation of the Spirit of God (*I Corinthians* 2.13, 14).

Paul knew and used the old Jewish idea that the Spirit of God both reveals God's truth and enables a man to recognise God's truth when it is revealed to him. But it was clear to Paul that the man who shut his heart to the Spirit, the man who refused to wait prayerfully and patiently and expectantly until he had received the Spirit, could not possibly receive or recognise God's truth. Even if it came to him, he would not recognise it as God's truth, for the Spirit is revealer and interpreter in one.

We are well aware that over-simplification can be dangerously easy and can in fact drift into heresy; but it is not altogether wrong to say that for Paul God the Father was God in creation, in recreation and in providence; that God the Son was God for ever and through all eternity active in redemption and in the saving of men; and that God the Holy Spirit is God for ever revealing his truth and conveying his power to men. Certainly to Paul the Holy Spirit is God's agent in revelation. We may put it this way. Externally, the Holy Spirit is the agent who brings God's truth to men; internally, the Holy Spirit is the person and the power who prepares men's hearts to receive that truth, and who enlightens their minds to comprehend and to understand it, and who enables and inspires them to pass it on to others.

We may put this in a wider way. The Holy Spirit is God's mediator; the Holy Spirit is the person who brings and who distributes God's gifts to men. It is the Holy Spirit who sheds abroad the love of God within our hearts (*Romans* 5.5). It is the Holy Spirit who leads and guides us into true sonship of God (*Romans* 8.14). It is by the Holy Spirit that we have access to the Father (*Ephesians* 2.18).

In this connection there are two conceptions of exceeding beauty in the thought of Paul.

In *Romans* 8.16 Paul writes : " The Spirit himself beareth witness with our spirit, that we are the children of God." In *Galatians* 4.6 (cp. *Romans* 8.15) he writes that because we are sons, God has sent forth the Spirit of his Son, into our hearts, crying, Abba, Father.

There is a most beautiful idea behind this. What gives us the certainty that we are the sons of God? What moves us to look up to God, and to cry, Father? How, even if we have a wistful desire to take it, can we be sure that the way is open to us to God? Even if there are the deepest longings in our hearts that it should be so, how can we be sure that the God to whom we look up is Father? Paul's answer is that the impulse which moves us in the first place to desire these things is the impulse of the Spirit. And the certainty in our hearts that we will not be disappointed is also the work of the Spirit. It is the Spirit who tells us of our need of God; it is the Spirit who starts us on the way to God; it is the Spirit who makes us sure that God is waiting to welcome us, and that he is the Father whom our hearts desire.

Paul's second idea in this connection is perhaps even more beautiful. In *Romans* 8.26 Paul writes, as the Authorized Version has it : " Likewise the Spirit also helpeth our infirmities : for we know not what we should pray for as we ought : but the Spirit himself maketh intercession for us with groanings which cannot be uttered; and he that searcheth the hearts knoweth what is the mind of the Spirit, because he maketh intercession for the saints according to the will of God." Moffatt translates that passage : " So too the Spirit assists us in our weakness; for we do not know how to pray aright, but the Spirit pleads for us with sighs that are beyond words, and he who searches the human heart knows what is the mind of the Spirit, since the Spirit pleads before God for the saints." In his commentary on *Romans,* Dr. C. H. Dodd has an exposition of that passage which is one of the noblest and most beautiful that has ever been penned. When we pray, we know too little of the will and purposes of God ever to pray aright. All that we can really offer to God, the highest kind of prayer, is an inarticulate sigh of the human heart and spirit, but the Holy Spirit can take that inarticulate sigh and translate it for us in the presence of God. William James, the famous psychologist, once wrote : " Many reasons have been given why we should not pray, whilst others are given why we should. But in all this very little is said of the reason why we do pray. The reason why we pray is simply that we cannot help praying." As C. H. Dodd so magnificently puts it : " Prayer is the divine in us appealing to the God above us." Paul would have said that it is the Holy Spirit within us who awakens that unutterable longing for God. He would have said that, being men we know not what to pray for; we can only bring to God a deep sigh of the human heart, which the Holy Spirit interprets to God for us.

In every letter Paul makes it clear that it is his conviction that the Holy Spirit is the source of the christian life. The Holy Spirit helps our infirmities (*Romans* 8.26). It is through the power of the Spirit that we abound in hope (*Romans* 15.13). It is by the power of the Spirit that we are sanctified (*Romans* 15.16; *II Thessalonians* 2.13). The Spirit is the source of Paul's own power (*Romans* 15.19). In *I Corinthians* 6.9-11 Paul sets out the grim list of sins to which the Corinthians had once been subject; but they are washed, they are sanctified, they are justified in the name of the Lord Jesus and by the Spirit of our God.

The Holy Spirit is the source of the many gifts which are necessary for the administration of the day to day ordering of the christian Church (*I Corinthians* 12.4ff). All lovely qualities which adorn the christian life are the fruit of the Spirit (*Galatians* 5.22). Our change from glory to glory until we become like Christ is the work of the Spirit (*II Corinthians* 3.18). The fact that Christians can be built and fitted together until their fellowship can become the habitation of God is the work of the Spirit (*Ephesians* 2.22). The strength of character and of personality that the Christian can achieve is the work of the Spirit (*Ephesians* 3.16).

It can be seen that for Paul the beginning and the middle and the end of the christian life all depend upon the work of the Spirit. The development of the individual Christian and the perfecting of the Church both depend upon the Spirit. A man's call, a man's forgiveness, a man's growth in grace are all the product of the power of the Spirit.

There is something very suggestive here. Something new has been brought into the conception of the work of the Spirit of God. In the Old Testament and in Jewish thought there was much about the Spirit, but for the most part it is true to say that the power and action of the Spirit were connected with extraordinary and abnormal happenings. The great utterances and the great visions of the prophets, sudden manifestations of the splendour of God, were the work of the Spirit; but in the New Testament the Spirit has become even more precious, for the Spirit has become the moving, the controlling, and the upholding power for everyday life and for everyday action.

The heathen philosophers cried out for what they called " the medicine for the sick soul ". For Paul the power of the Spirit was that very medicine, for the Spirit cleansed men from sin, broke the chains that bound them, and gave them day to day strength and joy and hope and peace and power.

It is then easy to see how for Paul the great actions and

the great qualities of the christian life are all in the Spirit. The Kingdom of God is righteousness, peace and joy in the Holy Spirit (*Romans* 14.17). We pray in the Spirit (*Ephesians* 6.18). Christians love each other in the Spirit (*Colossians* 1.8). The gospel comes to men in the Holy Spirit (*I Thessalonians* 1.5). Even in the midst of persecution, the Thessalonians have joy in the Holy Spirit (*I Thessalonians* 1.6). The worship of the Christian is shared and offered in the Spirit (*Philippians* 3.3).

It is as if the Spirit is the atmosphere and the climate in which alone the great christian qualities can grow and in which alone the christian graces can flourish, and in which alone the activities of the Christian individual and the christian Church can be carried on.

It is no surprise therefore to find Paul identifying the Spirit with life. The Spirit is life because of righteousness, he writes in *Romans* 8.10. The Spirit is the power by which the Christian enters the christian life, and the power in which he lives the christian life. The Spirit is at one and the same time the source and the sustainer of life in the fully christian sense of the term.

When we think of what Paul says of the Spirit and attributes to the Spirit, it becomes clear that the things which are in the Spirit are the things which are in Christ. Paul was not a systematic theologian but a man whom Christ had found and a man who had found Christ, and who was seeking to share that experience with others. He was not primarily propagating a theology; he was seeking to share a religious experience. It is therefore not surprising to find Paul in the end simply saying : " The Lord is the Spirit " (*II Corinthians* 3.17). To him to live in the Spirit was to live in the presence of his risen and ever-living Lord. It would not be too much to say that for Paul the Spirit was the fulfilment of the promise of Christ that he would be with his men alway even unto the end of the world (*Matthew* 28.20).

XV

PAUL'S THINKING ABOUT SIN

G. K. Chesterton once laid it down that, whatever else is true about man it is certainly true that man is not what he was meant to be. With that dictum Paul would have completely agreed; and the reason for that situation is sin. There are some who would accuse Paul of being, as it were, obsessed with sin. But the fact is this—Paul uses the word *hamartia,* the commonest word for sin, 62 times in his letters; and of these 62 occurrences 48 are in *Romans*; and only 14 in all the other letters; and in the letter to the Philippians the word *hamartia* does not occur at all. It is obviously true to say that Paul saw with intensity the seriousness of sin, but it would be quite wrong to say that he had a morbid obsession with the idea of sin. Let us then see what Paul has to say of sin.

First and foremost, we must note that Paul insisted on the universality of sin. Sin was not to him something in which only some people are involved; it is not like a disease which strikes some, and which others escape. To Paul every man is involved in sin. Both Jews and Gentiles are under sin (*Romans* 3.9). All have sinned and come short of the glory of God (*Romans* 3.23). Sin is a universal human predicament.

For Paul that universality of sin was doubly proved. First, it was a fact of human experience. Second, it was a fact of history. To Paul all men were involved in the sin of Adam; that is the whole point of *Romans* 5. It is not that all men sin *as* Adam sinned; it is not that all men inherited from Adam the taint and the tendency to sin; it is that in Adam all men did actually sin. To us this is a strange argument. To a Jew it was perfectly natural. The Jew believed strongly in solidarity. To this day there are primitive tribes, and if you ask a man from one of these

tribes his name, he will not tell you his name; he will give
the name of his tribe. He is bound up in his tribe; he has no
separate existence; apart from the tribe he does not live.
Just in that same way, in Adam all men sinned.

Paul's proof of that is simple, and to a Jew quite logical.
Because Adam sinned, death entered into the world. Death
is the penalty of sin. Adam's sin was a direct breach of a
commandment of God. Where there is no commandment
there can be no sin. Now the Law was not in the world
until Moses came; therefore there could be no breach of the
Law; there could be no sin in that sense of the term. And
yet between Adam and Moses men still died. They had not
broken the Law, for there was no Law to break; and still
they died. Why? Because they had sinned in Adam; in
him they had actually committed sin.

That is the Pauline argument. For him the facts of
human experience, and the facts of history, demonstrated
the universality of sin. So then we begin with this fact that
all have sinned.

It is inevitable that Paul should closely connect the Law
and sin. There are two senses in which the Law, so to speak,
produced sin. The Law defines sin; where there is no law
there can be no sin; and in that sense the Law creates sin.
To take a simple modern example. For a long time it may
be quite legal to drive a motor car up and down a street in
either direction. Then new traffic regulations are laid
down, and a law is enacted whereby that street becomes a
one-way street. By the enacting of that law a quite new
breach of the law has been created. Before the passing of
the law it was perfectly legal to drive up or down that
street in either direction; now it is only legal to drive in one
direction, and to drive in the other direction is a newly
created breach of the law. From the legal point of view a
new sin has been created. So then without the law there
can be no sin. "By the Law is the knowledge of sin"
(*Romans* 3.20). "Scripture has shut up all under sin"
(*Galatians* 3.22). "Sin is not imputed when there is no
law" (*Romans* 5.13). "The Law entered that the offence
might abound" (*Romans* 5.20). Until the coming of the

Law, no one could break the Law, and therefore there is a sense in which the Law created sin.

But there is another, and a much more dangerous sense, in which the Law *provokes* sin. It is a characteristic of human nature that as soon as a thing is forbidden it becomes desirable. It is the grass on the other side of the fence that is always most succulent. That is what Paul discovered by bitter experience : " I had not known sin, but by the Law : for I had not known desire except the Law had said : Thou shalt not covet." Sin " took occasion " by the commandment. " Without the Law sin was dead; for I was alive without the Law once; but when the commandment came, sin sprang to life, and I died." The commandment which was designed for life effected death. It was through the commandment that sin took occasion to deceive Paul and to lead him to death (*Romans* 7.7-11). Here is the universal dilemma. The Law, which is meant to forbid and to control sin, provokes sin, because of the fatal fascination of the forbidden thing. C. H. Dodd quotes in illustration of this the famous passage from Augustine :

There was a pear-tree near our vineyard laden with fruit. One stormy night we rascally youths set out to rob it and carry our spoils away. We took off a huge load of pears—not to feast upon them ourselves, but to throw them to the pigs—though we ate just enough to have the pleasure of forbidden fruit. They were nice pears, but it was not the pears that my wretched soul coveted, for I had plenty better at home. I picked them simply to be a thief. The only feast I got was a feast of iniquity, and that I enjoyed to the full. What was it that I loved in that theft? Was it the pleasure of acting against the law, in order that I, a prisoner under rules, might have a maimed counterfeit of freedom, by doing with impunity what was forbidden, with a dim similitude of omnipotence? (*Confessions* 2.4-6).

It is a fact of experience that the human heart desires

the forbidden thing; and the law by forbidding a thing awakens the desire for it.

So then in a double sense sin and the law are inextricably connected. The Law defines sin, and, therefore in a sense, creates sin; the Law by forbidding a thing awakens a desire for it. As Paul insists, without the Law there can be no sin.

Since sin and the Law are so closely intertwined, it is clear that sin is disobedience. It was by one man's disobedience that the many were constituted sinners (*Romans* 5.19). Any man who was capable of rendering to God and to God's law a perfect obedience would never sin. We may put this in another way—sin means listening to oneself instead of listening to God.

As soon as we have disobeyed the voice of God, and sinned, another element enters into the situation. Through sin we *come short* of the glory of God (*Romans* 3.23). What does that mean? When we go back to the old story of creation we find that God made man in his own image, and his own likeness (*Genesis* 1.26). That is to say God made man to bear his own image, and therefore to reflect his own glory. Sin therefore is what keeps a man from being what he was meant to be and what he was created to be. Here we come at the basic meaning of *hamartia*. *Hamartia* was not originally an ethical word at all. It was, in fact, a word from shooting; and it meant *a missing of the target*. Sin is the failure to hit the target; sin is the failure to be what we were meant to be; sin is falling below one's own possibilities. The moment a man begins to disobey he begins to lose the image of God, and therefore falls short of what he was meant to be. Here is the very foundation in practice of the universality of sin. To fail to do one's best as workman, to fail to be as good a father, mother, son, daughter as one might have been, to fail to use and to develop the gifts of hand and eye and mind and brain that God has given us, in any way to fall short of the best that we could be is a sin. Disobedience to God means failure in life; and failure to hit the target is sin.

It is characteristic of any disease that when it obtains a

grip it spreads; and so does sin. Sin and the offence *abound* (*Romans* 5.20). Sin is like some trouble which is allowed to gain a grip. Weeds which are not eradicated seed themselves and spread ever more virulently. A source of infection which is not removed is a breeding ground of disease. A cancer, unless it is excised, grows and spreads and develops. There is in sin an extraordinary power of self-multiplication. It sweeps like an epidemic through life, when it has gained the smallest foothold.

As Paul saw it, in a double sense *sin begets death*. It does that in the moral and the spiritual sense. "Sin, taking occasion by the commandment, deceived me, and by it slew me " (*Romans* 7.11). "The body is dead because of sin " (*Romans* 8.10). Sin has a killing power. It kills goodness; it kills beauty; it kills human love and human fellowship; it kills conscience and it kills character. If a man allows sin to grip him, the end is that he is dead in sin.

But as Paul saw it, not only does sin beget moral and spiritual death; sin is also the cause of *physical death*. Paul's teaching is that, if there had been no sin, there would have been no death. Death came into the world by sin (*Romans* 5.12); sin reigned unto death (*Romans* 5.21). A man can be the servant of sin unto death or of obedience unto righteousness (*Romans* 6.16). The wages of sin is death (*Romans* 6.23). As Paul sees it, it is through sin, and because of sin, that death entered into the world. Sin is the destroyer of moral and spiritual and physical life.

Again and again Paul uses words which stress in vivid pictures the power and the grip of sin. Sin *reigns* unto death (*Romans* 5.21). The word for *reign* is *basileuein,* which comes from the noun *basileus* which means a *king*. Sin becomes a king, and men become its wretched subjects. Sin is like a *slavery*. The work of Christ is that we should no longer be the slaves (*douleuein*) of sin (*Romans* 6.6). In his pre-christian days the Christian was the *slave* (*doulos*) of sin (*Romans* 6.20). "Sin," says Paul, "shall not *have dominion* over you" (*Romans* 6.14). The word he uses is *kurieuein* and *kurios* was the title for the emperor, or for the master of a slave, and denotes ownership and supreme power. In his Christless days Paul saw himself as *sold into the power of sin* (*Romans* 7.14), like a slave, knocked down at an auction, and becoming the absolute property of his owner.

As our own experience has shown again and again, there is a tyranny and an enslavement in sin; the grip of sin can become unbreakable; a man may desperately desire, for instance, to free himself from a habit, and be quite unable to do so. He has become the slave, the property, the subject, the creature of sin.

Sin does not remain an external power outside a man. As Paul saw it, sin takes up its residence within a man, and occupies him as an enemy occupies a conquered country. He speaks of the sin that dwells (*oikein*) in him; he speaks of the sin in his members (*Romans* 7.20, 23). Sin is not simply an influence or a force; it is a kind of personal demonic power which invades a man and takes up its residence within him. It is in fact there that Paul's whole conception of the body and the flesh come in. Any invading enemy requires a bridgehead; it is the flesh which gives sin its bridgehead. The flesh is not simply the body; and the sins of the flesh are not simply the fleshly sins. Idolatry, hatred, strife, wrath, heresy are all sins of the flesh (*Galatians* 5.20). The flesh is human nature apart from God. And it is just there that sin obtains the bridgehead for the invasion whose end is the occupation of the human personality.

There are two further facts about sin in the Pauline view which we must fit into this scheme. First, sin is that which hinders the work of Christ and the spread of the gospel. Those who hinder Paul from bringing the message of God to the Gentiles fill up their sin, they bring their sin to its summit and to its fulness (*I Thessalonians* 2.16). Second, sin is the opposite of faith. "Whatsoever is not of faith is sin" (*Romans* 14.23). Now faith for Paul was total surrender to God; and therefore sin is anything which hinders a man's total surrender to God. Sin is that which opposes or lessens or obstructs the lordship of God and his Christ in the world or in the human heart.

It is not our task here to examine the words for particular sins, but there are certain general words for sin which Paul uses, each of which has its contribution to make to his total picture of sin.

Sin is *adikia*, and the sinful man is *adikos*. The normal Authorized Version translation of these two words is *unrighteousness* and *unrighteous*. We shall best see the meaning of these words, if we come at them from their opposite. In Greek ethics the good man, the righteous man, the just man is *dikaios*; and the man who is *dikaios* is defined as the man who gives both to gods and to men what is their due. Unrighteousness is the failure to give to God and to men what is their due. The unrighteous man is the man who fails in his duty to God and to men; he is the man who fails to give God his love and his obedience, and who fails to give men his charity and his service. Paul so describes the sinner in *Romans* 1.18; 1.29; 3; 5; 6; 13; 9.14; *I Corinthians* 6.1, 7, 8.

The words *adikia* and *adikos* are not uncommonly joined with the words *asebia* and *asebēs*. These words describe the *godless* man and his conduct. Sin is godlessness; it is the total disregard of God; it is treating God as if he did not exist. It is not atheism, for atheism does not believe that there is a God. Godlessness knows that there is a God—and totally disregards him; it is therefore even worse than atheism.

Sin is *anomia*; and the sinner is the *anomos* (*Romans* 6.19; 2.12; *I Corinthians* 9.21; *II Corinthians* 6.14). *Nomos* means *law*; and the sinner is the man who disobeys God's law. This word stresses the deliberation of sin; it describes the man who well knows the right, and who yet does the wrong.

Sin is a *parakoē* (*Romans* 5.19; *II Corinthians* 10.6). The Authorized Version translates this word *disobedience*. But there is a vivid picture in it. It comes from the verb *parakouein*. *Parakouein* originally meant to *mishear* or *to*

fail to hear. It could be used of the man who did not catch
something that someone else said, because it was indistinctly
spoken, or because he himself was deaf. Then it came to
mean *deliberately not to hear,* as it were, to close the ears
to. In the last analysis a man hears only what he wants
to hear; and sin means closing the ears to God in order to
listen to oneself.

Sin is *parabasis* and the sinner is *parabatēs* (*Romans* 2.23;
4.15; *Galatians* 3.19; *Hebrews* 2.2; *James* 2.9). *Parabasis*
literally means *a stepping across.* The picture is of a man
stepping across a line across which he has no right to step, of
a man invading forbidden territory, and crossing the bounds
of that which is right. Sin is the deliberate crossing of the
fence between right and wrong.

Sin is *paraptōma* (*Romans* 4.25; 5.15, 16, 17, 20; *Ephesians* 1.7; 2.1; 2.5). *Paraptōma* originally meant *a slip,* a
trip up, a blunder. Longinus, for instance, the Greek
literary critic, uses it for the blunders in style and taste of
which even the best authors are occasionally capable. It is
of all words for sin the least deliberate. It describes the
slip which a man may make when he is off his guard, when
he is not looking where he is going, when he takes his eye
off the goal. Sin is the failure in concentration, the failure
in self-control through which a man is swept or slips into
sin.

Sin results in *pōrōsis* (*Romans* 11.7; 11.25; *II Corinthians* 3.14; *Ephesians* 4.18). *Pōrōsis* describes a process of
petrifaction, resulting in the complete loss of all sensation
and of all ability to feel. As Burns said of sin : " It petrifies
the feelings." If a man goes on sinning he kills his sense of
decency and honour and goodness; he comes to a stage
when regret and remorse and penitence are dead. It is the
progressive hardening of the heart, until the heart can no
longer respond in obedience to God and in compassion to
men.

Finally, there are two things to be put against all this.
First, grace is the antidote to sin. Where sin abounds grace
still further abounds (*Romans* 5.20). There is a power

which can check sin; and there is a power which can liberate from sin; and that power is grace; and grace is even greater than sin. Second, in spite of sin God has never ceased to love men. God commends his love to us, in that while we were yet enemies, Christ died for us (*Romans* 5.8). There is a love which will not let us go, and which will go even to the Cross to conquer sin—and therein lies our hope.

XVI

PAUL'S CONCEPTION OF THE FLESH

Any examination of the mind of Paul which failed to seek to understand what Paul meant by the flesh would be very inadequate, for this expression occurs again and again in his letters. At the same time the most cursory reading of Paul's letters makes it plain that it is not easy to understand just what Paul did mean by this word, for he very obviously does not use it always in the same way. He uses it in many different connections and with many different connotations, although it is true to say that among the many uses of it, there is one use which is characteristic of the mind and thought of Paul.

We have only to glance at a saying like *II Corinthians* 10.3 to see the difficulty. There Paul writes : Though we walk *in the flesh* (*en sarki*), we do not war *after the flesh* (*kata sarka*). It is quite clear that in that one sentence Paul is using the word *flesh* with widely differing meanings, although these meanings may be inter-related. *To walk in the flesh* is something which no man can avoid; *to war after the flesh* is something which every man must avoid. Let us then see if we can disentangle the various Pauline uses of the word flesh, *sarx*.

Paul frequently uses the word flesh in a quite neutral and literal sense, meaning nothing other than the human body. He tells us that his first visit to Galatia and his first preaching there were due to infirmity of the flesh (*Galatians* 4.13). That simply means that his first arrival in Galatia was due to some bodily ailment, some physical illness. He speaks of the thorn in his flesh (*II Corinthians* 12.7). The overwhelming probability is that the thorn in his flesh was a physical disability which caused him intense and excruciating pain. He speaks of being absent in the flesh (*Colossians* 2.5), and of those who have never seen his face in the

flesh (*Colossians* 2.1). He is referring there to those who
did not know him personally, and who had never seen him
face to face in the physical presence. He speaks of living in
the flesh and abiding in the flesh (*Philippians* 1.22, 24). He
is referring to the bodily, physical life which he lives.
When he speaks of Jesus, he speaks of the body of his flesh
(*Colossians* 1.22) by which he means the natural, physical
human body which Jesus wore in his days upon earth. He
speaks of the christian duty of ministering to those who are
poor in carnal things (*Romans* 15.27). The word is the
corresponding adjective *sarkikos*. *Carnal* is an unfortunate
translation, because it is a word which in English has acquired a bad connotation. When Paul speaks of ministering to the carnal needs of those who are less fortunate, he
simply means the duty of bringing practical help for everyday life and living to those who are poor and hungry and
who never have enough. In *I Corinthians* 9.27 he speaks
about keeping his body under, and of bringing it into subjection; and, if that passage be read in its context, its meaning is that throughout the long, weary and hard years he
had taught and disciplined himself to do without the luxur-
ies and the refinements, the indulgences and the softnesses,
which he might well have had and enjoyed.

We shall see later that when Paul speaks of the sins of the
flesh he is thinking of far more than sexual sins, that in fact
those sins are a very small part, and not the most important part, of sins of the flesh. But in *I Corinthians* 7.28 he
speaks of those who have trouble in the flesh, where the
reference is to the problem of continence in a difficult and a
dangerous situation.

Paul frequently uses the conception of the flesh when he
wishes to speak of things from what we might call the
purely human angle, when he is considering things from
the human and not from the divine point of view. Usually
there is no kind of condemnation, not even any kind of
criticism, involved.

Very often Paul uses the phrase *the flesh* just as we might
say *humanly speaking*. So Jesus was born of the seed of
David according to the flesh (*Romans* 1.3). That is to say,

looked at from the human angle, Jesus was a descendant of David. He lays it down that no flesh shall be justified in the sight of God by deeds of the Law (*Romans* 3.20). Here no flesh simply means no human being. He speaks of Abraham our father as pertaining to the flesh (*Romans* 4.1). That is simply to say that it is from Abraham that the Jews trace their physical descent. In *Ephesians* 6.5 he urges servants to be obedient to those who are their masters after the flesh. There he is drawing the distinction between those who are their human masters and God who is their heavenly Lord.

In *Galatians* 1.16 he says that after his conversion he did not confer with flesh and blood. That is to say, he did not seek counsel and advice from any merely human authority. In *II Corinthians* 1.17 he speaks of a purpose according to the flesh, that is, a purely human purpose. In *Philippians* 3.3, 4 he claims that, if anyone has grounds for glorying in the flesh, he has more. That is to say, if it comes to a contest on the grounds of human achievement and human qualifications, he can stand comparison with any man, and emerge victorious from the comparison. In *II Corinthians* 11.18 he speaks of those who glory after the flesh, that is, those who stake their claims for honour and for authority on purely human achievements and on purely human grounds.

This is in fact one of the commonest of all uses of the word flesh in Paul's letters. It does not confer or imply any kind of rebuke or condemnation. It merely states things in purely human terms apart from the divine plan and purpose.

Paul has two uses of the word flesh at which we may glance in the passing, because they are interesting and illuminating. In one case he uses the word almost in the sense of *pre-christian*. In *Romans* 7.5 he uses the expression " when we were in the flesh ". In its context that means before we met Christ, when we were struggling along defeatedly in our own strength and before we found peace and power in Jesus Christ. It is as if Paul looked at life in two stages. In the first stage he was in the flesh trying to deal with things in his own strength, and meeting with nothing but frustration. In the second stage he was in Christ, and was experiencing all the victorious blessedness which being in Christ brings with it.

The other instance is when he uses the allied word *sarkikos,* which the Authorized Version translates *carnal,* in the sense of *sub-christian.* In *I Corinthians* 3.3 he demands of the Corinthians : " Are you not carnal (*sarkikoi*)?" The reason of the demand is that they are still living in a quarrelsome, divided, sectarian existence, which is far below the standard of the life which those who are in Christ should live. They are living a sub-christian life.

We now arrive at the characteristically Pauline usage of the word flesh. In the mind of Paul the flesh is inextricably connected with sin. In this sense the word flesh has lost its physical meaning and has acquired an ethical meaning. In *Romans* 7.14 he says that in the days before he met Christ, he was carnal (*sarkinos,* another allied adjective) and sold under sin. In *Romans* 7.23-25 there is the agonised cry of the sick soul, which ends with the heart-breaking dilemma : " So then with the mind I myself serve the law of God; but with the flesh the law of sin." In *Romans* 8.6 to be carnally minded (literally, the habit of mind of the flesh) is death. In *Romans* 8.7 that same habit of mind is enmity against God. In *Romans* 8.12, 13 to live after the flesh is to die.

In *Romans* 13.14 Paul urges his people to make no provision for the flesh and for the lusts thereof. In *Galatians* 5.13 he insists that the Galatians must not use their freedom as an occasion for the flesh. In *Galatians* 5.17 flesh and spirit are wholly opposed. In *II Corinthians* 7.1 he speaks of the filthiness of the flesh. Here the flesh is integrally connected with sin.

It is here that we must be careful to note one all-important fact. When Paul thinks of the lust of the flesh, he is by no means thinking only, or even mainly, of the grosser sins, the sins which in our modern terminology are the sins of the flesh. Certainly he includes them, but they are not the principal sins of the flesh. In *Galatians* 5.19, 20 we have the list of the sins of the flesh. That list includes adultery, fornication, lasciviousness, uncleanness; but it also includes hatreds, variance, emulations, wrath, strife, envyings, murder, drunkenness, and even heresies.

It is quite clear that for Paul it is not only the fleshly sins which have their seat in the flesh; it is there that what we would call the spiritual sins also have their seat and their origin. It is of the greatest importance to note this.

We must bring in here another and a parallel Pauline conception—the conception of the old man. In *Ephesians* 4.22 Paul exhorts his people to put off the old man which is corrupt according to deceitful lusts. There are two parallel passages which together show how closely interconnected are the conceptions of the flesh and of the old man. In *Romans* 6.6 Paul writes : " Knowing this, that our old man is crucified with him, that the body of sin might be destroyed, that henceforth we should not serve sin." And in *Galatians* 5.24 Paul writes : " They that are Christ's have crucified the flesh with the affections and lusts." The parallelism is so close that it is clear that for Paul the flesh and the old man stand for one and the same thing; they stand for the helpless subjection to sin which dominates life before Christ enters it.

We must now ask what is in Paul's mind when he speaks of the flesh, and when he so closely connects the flesh and sin. Was this connection the outcome of the normal Greek dualism of the world in which Paul lived? The thinking Greeks were dominated by the conviction that matter is essentially evil, that matter as such is flawed and debased. With that conviction the Greeks could not do otherwise than think of the body as essentially evil; they were bound to long for the day when they would be rid of the body once and for all.

For the Greek the flesh of the body is the prison-house of the soul; the whole material universe is evil, and spirit alone is good. That is why the greatest of the Greeks believed in the immortality of the soul but would have been shocked at the idea of the resurrection of the body. To the Greek the body was an unmitigated evil. It was this idea which produced the Orphic jingle in the words: *Sōma sēma*, the body is a tomb. Plotinus, the neo-platonist, could say that he was ashamed that he had a body. Seneca could break out : " I am a higher being, and born for higher things than to be a slave of my body, which I look upon as only a shackle put upon my freedom . . . In so detestable a habitation dwells the free soul " (*The Moral Letters,* 65.20). Epictetus could say : " Thou art a poor soul burdened with a corpse."

Is this the basis of the Pauline conception of the flesh? When Paul connected the flesh with sin, was he simply taking over the Greek conception of the essential evil of all material and bodily things, and the essential supremacy of spirit?

The answer to that question must be an uncompromising no. Paul was very far from holding such a view of the body. To Paul the body was a noble instrument made for noble things. The heathen with their unclean ways dishonour the body (*Romans* 1.24), therefore the body itself is an honourable thing. A fornicator sins against his body (*I Corinthians* 6.18). Sexual impurity is a sin against the body which was made for purity. In *I Corinthians* 12 Paul works out his greatest picture of the Church, when he calls it the body of Christ. In *Romans* 12.1 he urges his people to present their bodies a living sacrifice, holy and acceptable to God—an idea which could never have entered the mind of a Greek, and which a Greek would have regarded with revulsion. In *I Corinthians* 3.16 and 6.19 Paul insists that the body is the temple of the Holy Spirit, and in *II Corinthians* 6.16 that it is actually the temple of God.

I Corinthians 15 deals with the resurrection of the body, an idea which, as we have seen, would be not only incredible but actively disgusting to a Greek. The Holy Spirit will quicken the mortal body (*Romans* 8.11). The body itself is to be redeemed (*Romans* 8.23). The body is to be conformed to Christ's glorious body (*Philippians* 3.21).

Paul's conception of the flesh comes from no other source than that of human experience. It is, in point of fact, by sense impressions that sin enters in. It is in point of fact the primitive basic instincts of the body which give sin its chance and its means of approach. It is these things, these tendencies which are the weapons and the instruments of sin. The Jewish Rabbis knew this. "The hand and the eye," they said, "are the two brokers of sin." "Passions lodge in the heart only of him who sees." As A. H. McNeile put it, it is true that the body is in actual fact "the handle and instrument of sin".

The New Testament several times uses a very vivid word; once in *Galatians* 5.13 Paul actually uses it in conjunction with the word flesh; the word is *aphormē*. An *aphormē* is what we would call in military language a bridgehead. An *aphormē* is the point at which an attack can be launched with the greatest possibility of success. *Aphormē* is, of course, frequently used in its literal sense; but it can also be used in a metaphorical sense. Dionysius of Halicarnassus (8.2, 5) tells how Coriolanus went to Tullus Attius to plot an insurrection which would lead him to power. He suggested how a certain situation could be deliberately provoked, a situation which could be used as a ground (*aphormē*) for just resentment. The situation would supply a bridgehead, a starting-point, an occasion, an opportunity to launch the contemplated attack.

What Paul has in mind when he speaks of the flesh is that the body with all its instincts, mental, emotional and physical, is the bridgehead where sin can launch its attack with the greatest prospect of success. That is why Paul can speak of the body of sin (*Romans* 6.6); the body of this death (*Romans* 7.24). That is why the body is dead because of sin (*Romans* 8.10), and why it is the body of our humiliation (*Philippians* 3.21).

When Paul spoke of the flesh he was thinking simply in terms of universal human experience. The body is capable of, and meant for, the highest and the greatest and the purest things; yet empirically and in actual practice the body is the seat of the passions and emotions which lead to sin, and which give sin its opportunity.

It is here that we gain our clue to the whole matter. We began by quoting *II Corinthians* 10.3 : "We walk *in the flesh* (*en sarki*), but we do not war *after the flesh* (*kata sarka*)." *En sarki,* in the flesh, we must be; *kata sarka,* after the flesh, we need not be. When the old man is crucified with Christ, when we have died to the old life and risen to the new life, we are still *en sarki,* in the flesh, but we are no longer *kata sarka,* after the flesh, for the Spirit of Christ is in us, so that we no longer walk according to the flesh but we walk according to the Spirit. "The life which I now live in the flesh," says Paul, "I live by the faith of the Son of God" (*Galatians* 2.20). All the instincts, the passions, the emotions, the desires which were the raw material of sin when they were controlled by our own human power become the raw material of goodness when they are controlled by Christ.

For Paul the flesh stood for all the weakness, all the inadequacy, all the liability to sin, which are inherent in human nature without Christ. The idea is the helplessness, the fallibility, even the sinfulness, of human nature without Christ. It is the Christless human nature which is helpless in the face of temptation. It is the human nature which is not only helpless in the face of temptation but which is—to use a Scottish word—thirled to sin. Calvin wrote : "Whatever is not in Christ, Paul calls flesh." C. H. Dodd writes : "The flesh is the common stuff of human nature which we inherit. Paul . . . does not think of it as necessarily evil but as powerless for moral ends." The flesh is man apart from God. Karl Barth asks : "What indeed does flesh mean but the complete inadequacy of the creature when he stands before his creator?"

So in this matter we see Paul doing what he so often and so rightly did. He is arguing from experience. He was not a theologian who had "never looked out of the window". He was not one of these writers who have ink in their veins instead of blood. He was not interested in abstruse and recondite speculations about the body. He never thought and never meant to say that, as the Greeks believed, the body was essentially an evil thing. By his own bitter experience he had discovered—as all must discover—that the Christless man has in his body a bridgehead through which sin can effect an entry into his life with fatal ease. But when a man's old self dies, and Christ springs to life within him, not only is his soul saved but his body also becomes the temple of the Holy Spirit. The man into whose inmost being Jesus Christ has entered is redeemed in body and in soul, and the body which was once the instrument of sin becomes the weapon of righteousness. It was not the destruction of the body, but the redemption of the body, for which Paul hoped and laboured and prayed.

XVII

THE SECOND COMING
IN THE THOUGHT OF PAUL

We do well to try to see what place the doctrine of the Second Coming had in the thinking of the early Church; for this is a doctrine which has suffered one of two opposite fates in the thought of the modern Church. For the most part, it is very largely disregarded; it is but seldom that a sermon upon it is heard; it is not too much to say that in many quarters it has come to be looked upon as one of the eccentricities of the faith, which have been outgrown and left behind. On the other hand there are some few who think about hardly anything else; the Second Coming to them is the most important doctrine in the christian faith; it dominates all their thinking and all their preaching. It is of extreme importance that we should try to adjust the balance, and that we should see both that the doctrine of the Second Coming receives its just place in our thinking, and that it does not usurp a place that is not its own, until it fills the whole horizon.

It is always of importance to see not only where christian thought ends, but also where it begins. To a Jew the doctrine of the Second Coming would have seemed not only completely intelligible, but even completely inevitable. We do not say that the doctrine of the Second Coming is a product of Jewish thought for no one can honestly read the gospels and fail to admit that Jesus did speak of his Coming in power; but we do say that the pictures in which the Second Coming were visualised were very largely Jewish both in their outline and in their detail.

It is possible to regard Jewish thought in two ways. In one sense the Jews were the greatest pessimists in history; but in a far truer sense the Jews were the greatest optimists in history. The Jews never lost the conviction that they

were the Chosen People. To them that chosenness necessarily implied world respect, world power, and world domi-
nation. It became increasingly clear to them that the triumph to which they looked forward could never happen by
purely human means; it must happen by the direct intervention of God into world affairs. Their numbers were too
few for them ever to reach world power; there were only
about four million Jews in Palestine in the time of Jesus,
and that was as nothing compared with the world empires.
They had lost their independence. They were subject in
turn to the Babylonians, the Persians, the Greeks and the
Romans. If God's promise, as they saw it, was ever to come
true, it could only come true by direct, supernatural and
divine intervention in human affairs. To that intervention
the Jew looked forward, and still looks forward.

In the thought of the Jew that idea took a basic and
fundamental form. The Jew divided all time into two ages.
There was *this present age,* which was wholly evil, wholly
wicked, and wholly bad. It was beyond cure; it could only
be cured by being destroyed, annihilated and obliterated.
There was *the age to come,* which would be the golden age
of God.

How was the one age to become the other? How was
this fundamental change to be effected? The change was
to come through *the Day of the Lord.* The Day of the Lord
would be the day of the intervention of God; it would be
a day of cosmic agony, the day of the birth-pangs of the
emergence of a new universe. Let us look first of all at the
Jewish dream of the golden age.

The golden age would be an age of plenty, an age when
earth would bring forth her fruits in such munificent and
effortless abundance that all would have enough and none
would have too little. " Behold, the days come, saith the
Lord, that the ploughman shall overtake the reaper, and
the treader of grapes him that soweth seed; and the mountains shall drop sweet wine, and all the hills shall melt . . .
And they shall plant vineyards, and drink the wine thereof;
they shall also make gardens, and eat the fruit of them "
(*Amos* 9.13, 14). " The wilderness shall be a fruitful field,

and the fruitful field be counted for a forest " (*Isaiah* 32.15).
" The Lord will comfort all her waste places; and he will
make her wilderness like Eden, and her desert like the
garden of the Lord " (*Isaiah* 51.3).

It would be an age of friendship; in particular it would
be an age when the enmity between man and the beasts
would no longer exist. " In that day will I make a covenant for them with the beasts of the field, and with the fowls
of heaven, and with the creeping things of the ground :
and I will break the bow and the sword and the battle out
of the earth, and will make them to lie down safely "
(*Hosea* 2.18). " The wolf also shall dwell with the lamb, and
the leopard shall lie down with the kid; and the calf and the
young lion, and the fatling together; and a little child shall
lead them. And the cow and the bear shall feed; their
young ones shall lie down together and the lion shall eat
straw like the ox. And the sucking child shall play on the
hole of the asp, and the weaned child shall put his hand on
the cockatrice' den; they shall not hurt nor destroy in all
my holy mountain " (*Isaiah* 11.6-9). In the golden age
there would be a friendship which would cover all living
things throughout all the earth.

In the golden age there would be no more pain; it would
be the land of the ever young, what in Gaelic the High-
landers call Tir-nan-og. " There shall be no more thence
an infant of days, nor an old man that hath not filled his
days : for the child shall die an hundred years old "
(*Isaiah* 65.20). A man's life would be like the life of a tree
for years (*Isaiah* 65.22). " The inhabitant shall not say, I
am sick " (*Isaiah* 23.24). " He will swallow up death in
victory; and the Lord God will wipe away tears from off all
faces " (*Isaiah* 25.8). There would be no more pain, and no
more death too soon.

The golden age would be the age of peace, the age when
wars would be no more. " They shall beat their swords into
ploughshares, and their spears into pruning-hooks : nation
shall not lift up sword against nation, neither shall they
learn war any more " (*Isaiah* 2.4). " They shall not hurt
nor destroy in all my holy mountain " (*Isaiah* 11.9). " My

people shall dwell in a peaceable habitation, and in sure dwellings, and in quiet resting places" (*Isaiah* 32.18). "Great shall be the peace of thy children" (*Isaiah* 54.13). The terror of war would be for ever gone.

We must now go on to ask : What would be the place of the people of Israel in this new universe of God? There is no one answer to that question.

It was universally believed that Jerusalem would be the centre of the world, and to her all the nations would come to learn the ways of God. "And it shall come to pass in the last days, that the mountain of the Lord's house shall be established in the top of the mountains, and shall be exalted above the hills; and all nations shall flow unto it. And many people shall go and say, Come ye, and let us go up to the mountain of the Lord, to the house of the God of Jacob; and he will teach us of his ways, and we will walk in his paths : for out of Zion shall go forth the law, and the word of the Lord from Jerusalem" (*Isaiah* 2.2, 3; *Micah* 4.1, 2). Jerusalem was to be the religious centre of the world. To her all men would come to find God.

Some few, some very few, of the Jews, had the noblest of all dreams—the dream that the Jews must go out to the world to bring to all men the knowledge of God, that the Jews had a missionary duty, that they were meant by God to be a light to the Gentiles. "I will give thee for a light to the Gentiles, that thou mayest be my salvation unto the end of the earth" (*Isaiah* 49.6). "The glory of the Lord shall be revealed, and all flesh shall see it" (*Isaiah* 40.5). This was a dream which came to only very few. The missionary task was a task to which the vast majority of the Jews were blind.

The commonest dream of all was the dream of power, the dream of conquest, the dream of a day when all men would be subjected to a world empire of the Jews. "The nation and kingdom that will not serve thee shall perish; yea, those nations shall be utterly wasted" (*Isaiah* 60.12). "The labour of Egypt, and merchandise of Ethiopia and of the Sabeans, men of stature, shall come over unto thee, and they shall be thine : they shall come after thee; in

chains they shall come over, and they shall fall down unto
thee" (*Isaiah* 45.14). "And it shall be, that whoso will not
come up of all the families of the earth unto Jerusalem to
worship the King, the Lord of hosts, even upon them shall
be no rain. And if the family of Egypt go not up, and
come not, that have no rain, there shall be the plague,
wherewith the Lord will smite the heathen that come not
up to keep the feast of tabernacles" (*Zechariah* 14.17, 18).

We must now turn our thoughts to the way in which the
change would be brought about. Broadly speaking, Jewish
thought envisaged two ways in which this change would
take place.

There was a time when the Jews believed that this change
would take place under human leadership. In the days
before they had realised their own smallness and their own
helplessness, in the days before their successive captivities
had convinced them that human power would never raise
them to greatness, their dream had always been that a great
leader and commander would arise from the stock of David,
and lead them to world greatness. "And there shall come
forth a rod out of the stem of Jesse (David was the son of
Jesse), and a Branch shall grow out of his roots" (*Isaiah*
11.1). "Then there shall enter in by the gates of this
house, kings sitting upon the throne of David" (*Jeremiah*
22.4). "They shall serve the Lord their God, and David
their king whom I will raise up unto them" (*Jeremiah*
30.9). "Behold, the days come, saith the Lord, that I will
raise unto David a righteous Branch, and a king shall reign
and prosper, and shall execute judgment and justice in the
earth" (*Jeremiah* 23.5). It was of this that men were thinking when in the gospel story they addressed Jesus as Son of
David (*Luke* 18.38; *Matthew* 21.9).

But, as we have said, the Jews became convinced that no
human power could ever bring in the new age, and that it
could only come through the direct intervention of God in
history. And hence there arose the conception of The Day
of the Lord which pervades so much of the Old Testament.
The Day of the Lord was to be the day of God's direct

intervention; it was to be a day of concentrated dread, the birth-pangs of the new age. Let us now look at the characteristics which in Jewish thought marked the Day of the Lord.

It was to be a day of destruction and of terror. "Behold the day of the Lord cometh, cruel both with wrath and fierce anger, to lay the land desolate" (*Isaiah* 13.9). "Alas for the day! for the day of the Lord is at hand, and as a destruction from the Almighty shall it come" (*Joel* 1.15). "That day is a day of wrath, a day of trouble and distress, a day of wasteness and desolation, a day of darkness and gloominess, a day of clouds and thick darkness" (*Zephaniah* 1.15). The whole terror of God was to be unleashed on the wickedness of the world.

It was to be a day of cosmic upheaval, when the world would be shaken and shattered to its very foundations. "And I will shew wonders in the heavens and in the earth, blood, and fire, and pillars of smoke. The sun shall be turned into darkness, and the moon into blood, before the great and the terrible day of the Lord" (*Joel* 2.30, 31). "For the stars of heaven and the constellations thereof shall not give their light : the sun shall be darkened in his going forth, and the moon shall not cause her light to shine . . . Therefore I will shake the heavens, and the earth shall remove out of her place, in the wrath of the Lord of Hosts, and in the day of his fierce anger" (*Isaiah* 13.10, 13). The day of the Lord would be a violent dissolution of the established world.

It would be a day of judgment, when the wicked would be sought out and finally obliterated. "I will punish the world for their evil, and the wicked for their iniquity; and I will cause the arrogance of the proud to cease, and will lay low the haughtiness of the terrible" (*Isaiah* 13.11).

So far we have taken all our evidence from the pages of the Old Testament itself. But in the days between the Old and New Testaments, many Jewish books were written concerning this time of terror which would be the prelude to the new age. These books are called Apocalypses; the

Greek word *apokalupsis* means an *unveiling* or a *revealing* and these books were visions of the end of this world and the beginning of the new world, visions of the intervention of God. We must remember that they were written in days when Israel was suffering terribly at the hands of her conquerors, and these books were the favourite reading matter of the people, for they foretold the end of Israel's misery and the beginning of her glory. They were books which Jesus would certainly know and which Paul would certainly have read.

In them the Old Testament characteristics of the Day of the Lord are repeated and still further accentuated. They foretold that there would be wars. There would be " quakings of places, tumults of peoples, scheming of nations, confusion of leaders, disquietude of princes" (*IV Ezra* 9.3). " There shall come astonishment of mind upon the dwellers on earth. And they shall plan to war one against another, city against city, place against place, people against people, kingdom against kingdom " (*IV Ezra* 13.31).

These books give even more terrifying pictures of the shaking of the world. " From heaven shall fall fiery swords, down to the earth. Lights shall come, bright and great, flashing into the midst of men; and earth, the universal mother, shall shake in those days at the hand of the Eternal; and the fishes of the sea and the beasts of the earth and the countless tribes of flying things and all the souls of men and every sea shall shudder at the presence of the Eternal and there shall be panic " (*The Sibylline Oracles* 3.363ff). " The horns of the sun shall be broken, and he shall be turned into darkness, and the moon shall not give her light, and be turned wholly into blood, and the circle of the stars shall be disturbed " (*The Assumption of Moses* 10.5).

One of the most terrible things would be a kind of complete destruction and reversal of all moral standards.

And honour shall be turned to shame,
And strength humiliated into contempt,
And probity destroyed,
And beauty shall become ugliness . . .

And envy shall rise in those who had not thought aught
of themselves,
And passion shall seize him that is peaceful,
And many shall be stirred up in anger to injure many,
And they shall rouse up armies in order to shed blood,
And in the end they shall all perish together with them
(*II Baruch* 27)

In the thought of the Old Testament and in the writings of the Jews between the Testaments, there is nothing more deeply rooted than the thought of the terrible coming of the Day of the Lord. It was in Judaism that Christianity was cradled; these were ideas on which every Jew fed his mind; it was only natural that there should be a kind of identification of the Day of the Lord and the Second Coming of Jesus Christ; both were the great intervention of God in human affairs. In christian thought the two became deeply intertwined. To the Christian the Second Coming of Jesus Christ was indeed the Day of the Lord.

With all that Jewish heritage in our minds we now turn directly to the New Testament. The Second Coming of Jesus Christ was always an essential part of the message of the christian Church. One of the most notable contributions to New Testament scholarship in modern times is C. H. Dodd's reconstruction of what is called the *kerugma*. The word *kerugma* literally means *a herald's announcement,* and it is used to describe the basic elements in the preaching of the early Church. As C. H. Dodd formulated them, on the basis of the sermons of the Book of Acts, and the Letters of Paul, these basic elements were :

The prophecies are fulfilled, and the new age has been inaugurated by the coming of Christ.
He was born of the seed of David.
He died, according to the Scriptures, to deliver us out of this present evil age.
He was buried.
He rose again on the third day, according to the Scriptures.

He is exalted at the right hand of God, as Son of
God, and Lord of the quick and the dead.

He will come again as judge and saviour of men.

That is to say, the Doctrine of the Second Coming of Christ
was from the beginning an integral and essential part of the
christian message.

The doctrine is there in *Acts* 1.11 in the announcement
of the two angelic figures : " This same Jesus, which is
taken up from you into heaven, shall so come in like manner
as ye have seen him go into heaven." It is there in Peter's
sermon : " That he may send the Messiah appointed before-
hand for you, Jesus, whom heaven must receive until the
time of the restoration of all things, of which God spake
through the mouth of his prophets from the beginning "
(*Acts* 3.21). In *Acts* 10.42 it is said that Jesus is appointed
to be the Judge of the quick and the dead.

In *Acts* there are only these three references to the Second
Coming in the account of the early preaching; but with
Paul it is different. It is the simple fact that in every one of
Paul's letters except *Galatians,* and possibly *Ephesians,* the
Second Coming is not only mentioned but stressed as an
essential part of the Christian gospel.

Before we go on to examine Paul's references to the
Second Coming in detail, we may note two special references to it. In *Romans* 2.16 Paul speaks of the day when
God shall judge the world by Jesus Christ " according to
my gospel ". The Second Coming was therefore an essential
part of that account of the gospel which Paul considered to
be uniquely his. When he is writing to the Thessalonians, he
beseeches them to live the christian life by the coming of
the Lord Jesus Christ, and by our gathering unto him (*II
Thessalonians* 2.1). The Second Coming was one of the
primary motives for the christian life. Apart from the many
other references, which we shall go on to consider, even
these two taken alone would serve to show how central the
idea of the Second Coming was to the thought and to the
teaching of Paul.

It is commonly said that Paul's conception of the Second

Coming underwent a certain development. It is true that Paul's ideas about the Second Coming did change, but it is not true that Paul, so to speak, grew out of the idea, or that he abandoned it. From the beginning to the end of Paul's life the idea was there. Let us go to his letters, and let us take soundings in them from the earliest to the latest. With the possible exception of the Letter to the Galatians, the letters to the Church at Thessalonica are Paul's earliest letters. There the Second Coming is set before men with vividness and with immediacy. One of the things which worried the Christians at Thessalonica was the problem of what was to happen to Christians who had died before the Second Coming arrived. Would they lose the glory which was bound to come to those who remained? Paul assures them that it will not be so : " For this we say unto you by the word of the Lord, that we which are alive and remain unto the coming of the Lord shall not take precedence of them that sleep " (*I Thessalonians* 4.15). When Paul wrote that, he obviously expected the Second Coming to happen within his own lifetime and within the lifetime of those to whom he was writing. In *I Thessalonians* 5.23 he writes that it is his prayer to God that their spirit, soul and body may be preserved blameless unto the coming of the Lord Jesus Christ. The significant thing there, is the mention of the body. The obvious implication is that he expected them to be in the body when Christ came; he expected the coming of Christ to be within their lifetime and his.

Let us turn now to *Romans*. In *Romans* 13.11, 12 there is that great passage in which Paul writes with a certain splendour of words : " And, knowing the time, it is now high time to awake out of sleep; for now is our salvation nearer than when we believed; the night is far spent, the day is at hand; let us therefore cast off the works of darkness, and let us put on the armour of light." In that passage the Second Coming is not mentioned in so many words; but the Second Coming is the whole background of it; and it is the imminence of the Second Coming which is the ground of the urgency of his appeal. But one thing is to be noted. That very passage is the culmination of the long passage in which Paul looks forward to the evangelisation of the whole world, Jewish and Gentile. All men were to hear the gospel; and all were to be given the chance to be gathered in. Clearly a process of evangelisation like that would take time; and we might think that by this time Paul did not expect the Second Coming to happen quite as soon as when he wrote to the Church at Thessalonica. But it is doubtful if we can lay a great deal of stress on that argument.

We now turn to *I Corinthians* 7 which is of paramount importance for this matter. The keynote of that passage is in *I Corinthians* 7.29 : " But this I say, brethren, the time is short." The passage comes in a discussion of marriage and of sexual relationship. Paul's verdict is that, if a man's natural passions are strong, and, if abstention from marriage is going to drive the man to the risk of immorality, then the man may marry; but, he would be much better not to; he would be better to avoid all earthly bonds and commitments so that he can concentrate the whole of life on preparation for the coming of Christ. The importance of that passage lies in this. Not only does it show that Paul at that time believed in the imminence of the Second Coming, but it shows that his advice to all men was to arrange and order life on the assumption that the Second Coming was going to happen at any moment.

We now turn to the last letters which Paul wrote. When he wrote the Letter to the Philippians the likelihood is that he was in his last imprisonment; and once again in it there comes the warning and the challenge : " The Lord is at hand " (*Philippians* 4.5). It has been said, and said truly, that the Letter to the Ephesians represents the highest reach of Pauline thought. It is indeed the Queen of the Epistles. Here is the fullest development of the thought of Paul. It is very commonly—almost universally—stated that in *Ephesians* there is no mention at all of the Second Coming, that by this time Paul had outgrown that whole conception. Is that completely true? In *Ephesians* 4.30 Paul speaks of the Holy Spirit " whereby ye are sealed unto the day of redemption ". Is not that at least possibly still another reference to the last great day of victory and of judgment in the Second Coming of Christ?

It is, we believe, demonstrable that from the first to the last letter which he wrote, the Second Coming is always in the mind of Paul, although it is less in the foreground at the end than it was at the beginning.

The Corinthian letters come in the midtime of Paul's ministry for Christ, and for this matter they are very important. In *I Corinthians* 10.11 he speaks of us on whom the ends of the world were come. In that age men were living—it does not matter how we put it for this purpose—in the last twilight of the old age, or the first dawn of the new. But by far the most significant saying comes at the very end of the first letter to the Corinthians in *I Corinthians* 16.22. There Paul writes : " If any man love not the Lord Jesus Christ, let him be anathema (accursed). *Maranatha.*" *Maranatha* is the Aramaic for The Lord is at hand, or for, Come, Lord !

Certain extremely important conclusions follow from this sentence. It comes right at the end of the letter, with only the blessing to follow. It is as if it was the culmination, the keystone, the heart of the message of Paul. It is as if he wished to leave the readers of the letter with that phrase ringing in their ears. It is almost as if he said : " Whatever else you remember or forget, never forget that the Lord is at hand." The very position of that sentence sets it, as it were, in bold type. Further, there is this. The Church at Corinth was a Greek Church; it could have had very few Jews in it at all; and yet, writing as he was to Greeks, Paul ends with this phrase in Aramaic. No Greek would know Aramaic; and yet the Greeks of Corinth must have understood this Aramaic phrase. Only one conclusion is possible; the phrase must have been a catchword, a slogan, a battle-cry, a watchword, a motto, which every Christian knew and understood.

This very expectation gave rise in Paul's letters to a phrase which with Paul is a characteristic description of the christian life. Again and again Paul speaks of the Christian as waiting for Jesus Christ. The christian life was essentially

nothing other than an expectation of and waiting for the
coming of Christ. He reminds the Thessalonians "how ye
turned to God from idols to serve the living and true God,
and to wait for his Son from heaven" (*I Thessalonians* 1.9,
10). He prays that the Lord may direct their hearts into the
patient waiting for Christ (*II Thessalonians* 3.5). He declared that the Thessalonians are to be his hope, his joy, his
crown of rejoicing in the presence of the Lord Jesus Christ
at his coming (*I Thessalonians* 2.19). He speaks of the
Corinthians as waiting for the coming of our Lord Jesus
Christ (*I Corinthians* 1.7). He tells the Philippians that our
conversation is in heaven from whence also we look for the
Saviour, the Lord Jesus Christ (*Philippians* 3.20).

We must note another important fact. When Paul did
speak of the Second Coming he often used language which
he had inherited from his Jewish scholarship and upbringing. In particular he was much influenced by the
twenty-sixth and twenty-seventh chapters of *Isaiah*. We
may note certain parallels.

1. The Lord's Coming : *Isaiah* 26.21; *II Thessalonians*
2.1.

2. The coming of judgment : *Isaiah* 26.21; *II Thessalonians* 1.9; 2.8.

3. The Resurrection of the dead : *Isaiah* 26.19; *I Thessalonians* 4.16.

4. The Sound of the trumpet : *Isaiah* 27.13; *I Thessalonians* 4.16.

5. The Gathering and Assembling of the Elect of God,
which was an essential part of the Jewish idea of the last
days : *Isaiah* 27.12; *I Thessalonians* 4.17.

It was inevitable that Paul should speak to people in
language and in pictures which they could understand; he
was bound to take his pictures from the Old Testament and
from the imagery of the end with which men were very
familiar.

But there is a warning here; it is quite clear that we
cannot approach these pictures with a crude literalism, that
we cannot take them to be an advance photographic record
of the events of the Second Coming. It is clear that they are

pictures of prophetic symbolism. The fact of the Second Coming they stress and lay down; but to take them as literal pictures of the details of the Second Coming is to forget that they come from the minds and the voices of the prophets, who used them only as symbols of the unspeakable terrors and glories which would be.

We have seen how integral the idea of the Second Coming was to the thought of Paul; and we have seen how Paul took many of his pictures of the Second Coming from the prophets and from his Jewish heritage. It will therefore not surprise us to find that one central Jewish idea occurs in Paul's thought in a new guise. We saw what a great part the idea of the Day of the Lord played in Jewish thought. In Paul's thought the Day of the Lord becomes the Day of Christ. He writes to the Thessalonians : "The Day of Christ is at hand " (*II Thessalonians* 2.2). It is his confidence that the Corinthians will be blameless in the Day of the Lord Jesus Christ (*I Corinthians* 1.8). They are to be his rejoicing in the Day of the Lord (*II Corinthians* 1.14). He tells the Philippians that, if they are worthy of their christian calling, he will have cause to rejoice in the Day of the Lord (*Philippians* 2.16). The Day of Christ was as essential a part of the thought of Paul, as the day of the Lord was of the thought of the Jews. Let us then see what Paul has to say about the Day of Christ.

Paul believed that the Day of Christ would come suddenly and without warning. "The Day of the Lord so cometh as a thief in the night " (*I Thessalonians* 5.2). That was not to say that it would not be preceded by signs (*II Thessalonians* 2). There would be a time of falling away, and a final contest with evil, but the actual moment of its coming would be shatteringly sudden.

The Day of Christ would be a day when the holy wrath of God would be let loose on a rebellious world. It is Paul's hope that his own people, Christ's people, will be found blameless (*I Thessalonians* 3.13; *I Corinthians* 1.8); but for the rebellious, and for those who are at enmity with God, it will be a day of dreadful punishment (*II Thessalonians* 1.7-10). In a sense that is why the Christian looks forward

to the Day of the Lord. On that day the righteous will find
their rest, and their persecutors will find the punishment
which their misdeeds have merited (*II Thessalonians* 1.6,
7). The Christian hope and joy are in the expectation of
that day (*I Thessalonians* 1.10); for, when Christ appears,
they too will appear in glory (*Colossians* 3.4).

Here is the place where we must face, not one of the
problems, but one of the great facts of Paul's scheme of
things. Paul believed intensely in judgment. It does not
matter whether Paul believed that that judgment would
come at the Day of the Lord, or whether it would be post-
poned to some later time; the essential fact is that Paul
gave a very real place to judgment in the christian scheme
of things. In *Romans* 2.5 he speaks of that day of wrath and
revelation, when God will render to every man according
to his deeds. In *Romans* 2.16 he speaks of the day when
God will judge the secrets of men by Jesus Christ. In
Romans 5.9 he speaks of the Christian being saved from
the wrath by the work of Jesus Christ. *I Corinthians* 4.5
speaks of the folly of judging until the Lord who is to come
will judge the secret things of the hearts of men. In
Colossians 3.24, 25 Paul urges men to do everything as unto
the Lord, knowing that of the Lord they will receive the
reward of the inheritance . . . but that he who does wrong
will receive for that which he has done, without respect of
persons. *Ephesians* 6.8 counsels fine living, in the knowledge that whatsoever good thing any man does, the same
shall he receive of the Lord. *I Corinthians* 3.13 declares
that every man's work will be judged. *I Corinthians* 3.17
declares that he who defiles the temple of God will pay the
penalty. *I Corinthians* 5.13 extends this judgment to
those who are without; it will be a universal judgment.
II Corinthians 5.10 says bluntly that we must all
appear before the judgment seat of Christ, that every man
may receive the things done in his body, whether they be
good or bad. And then Paul goes on to say that it is knowing the terror of the Lord, that we do persuade men. In
Romans 14.10 he lays it down that we shall all stand before
the judgment seat of Christ.

Judgment is an essential principle of the christian faith. This has caused many people difficulty. What has grace to do with judgment? If Christianity is a religion of grace, if forgiveness is utterly free, utterly unmerited, utterly undeserved, the product of nothing other than the love and mercy of God, and, if this grace is so superabundant that, wherever sin abounds, it abounds still more, what place is left for judgment? If a man must be judged by the deeds done in his body, what has happened to justification by faith? If no flesh can ever be justified by deeds, how then can a man finally be judged by deeds? These are questions which demand an answer.

First, Paul was cradled in Judaism, and Judaism is an intensely ethical religion. It offered a way of life; as Jesus himself said: "By their fruits shall ye know them" (*Matthew* 7.20). Even if he had wished to, Paul could never have escaped from the ethical demands of religious faith. And an ethical religion involves standards of judgment, from which there can be no escape. When a way of life is laid down, failure to live that way of life must have its inevitable consequence.

Second, Paul was a missionary. He lived and preached in a Gentile world which was notoriously immoral; he could not have gone out with any other message than that goodness was demanded from a Christian, and that evil is punished. No message other than the stern demand could have produced results.

Third, it is possible gravely to mis-state the doctrine of grace. Grace is the greatest gift in the world; but grace is the greatest responsibility in the world. Grace is a gift; and grace is a gift of love; to offer that grace to men cost God all he had to give; and therefore there is laid on every man the awe-inspiring obligation of doing all he can to deserve that grace. That he can never do; but he can and must respond to that grace by seeking throughout all his life to be what that grace desires him to be. He must say: "If I have been loved like that I dare not break the heart of that love." A man who fails to see the obligation of grace is a man who is blind to honour and blind to love; he has sinned against the greatest love in the universe. It is true that grace does everything; but to grace a man must respond. And if a man fails to respond, there must be consequences.

Fourth, it must be clearly understood that Justification by Faith is the beginning of the christian life. Through justification by faith a man is put into a right relationship with God; he learns and realises and glories in the fact that God is his friend and not his enemy. But that new relationship must issue in a new life; it must go on to sanctification, by which a man's life and living are changed. The whole point of that new relationship is to enable a man to live a life, where he can conquer sin and enter into the righteousness of Jesus Christ. He can only prove that he has entered into that relationship by seeking to live a life which fits that relationship. Long ago Nietzsche, the German atheist philosopher said : " Show me that you are redeemed, and I will believe in your redeemer." Justification, like grace, brings a man an immense privilege and lays on a man an immense responsibility. Judgment is an essential part of the christian faith for the very simple reason that Christianity is meant to make a man a certain kind of man, and enables him to be that kind of man; and, if he fails to be that kind of man, then there is only one conclusion—he is not really christian; and the fault is his, for the enabling grace was there.

Let us then sum up the ultimate values of the doctrine of the Second Coming.

It would help a great deal if first of all we would realise that we are in effect forbidden to speculate about its date and time. Jesus said : " Of that day and that hour knoweth no man, no, not the angels which are in heaven, neither the Son, but the Father " (*Mark* 13.32). To claim, or to aspire to, a knowledge of that of which Jesus himself was ignorant is nothing short of blasphemy. The fact of the Second Coming we must accept; of the method, the date, the time of it we are forbidden to speculate.

The great value of the doctrine of the Second Coming is that it guarantees that history is going somewhere. We cannot tell how it will happen, and when it will happen.

We cannot take as literal truth the Jewish pictures of it which Paul used. We need not think of a physical coming of Christ in the clouds, or a physical trumpet blast. But what the doctrine of the Second Coming conserves is the tremendous fact that there is one divine, far-off event to which the whole creation is moving; there is a consummation; there is a final triumph of God. In his book, *An Arrow into the Air*, John H. Withers has a quotation from Gerald Healy's play, *The Black Stranger*. It comes from the days of the Irish potato famine in 1846. At that time as part of the relief work men were set to making roads which had no purpose whatever. It was simply to give them some work to do. One day in that desperate situation Michael comes home to his father, and says with a kind of poignant disillusionment: "They're makin' roads that lead to nowhere!" When we confess our ignorance, an ignorance which even Jesus shared, of dates and times; when we abandon all the Jewish imagery and pictures, which by this time have become only fantastic; when we strip the doctrine of the Second Coming down to its bare essentials; we are left with this tremendous truth—the doctrine of the Second Coming is the final guarantee that life can never be a road that leads to nowhere; it is a road which leads to Christ.

XVIII

THE MIND OF PAUL
CONCERNING THE CHURCH

The letters of Paul provide us with ample material for arriving at a clear idea of his thoughts and beliefs concerning the Church; for in them the word *ekklēsia*, church, occurs about sixty times. Let us first see how, and in what connections, he uses this word.

Paul uses the word *ekklēsia*, both in the singular and in the plural, to describe the body of believers in any given place. So he speaks to the Church at Cenchrea (*Romans* 16.1); the Church of the Laodiceans (*Colossians* 4.16); the Church of the Thessalonians (*I Thessalonians* 1.1; *II Thessalonians* 1.1). He speaks of the Churches of the Gentiles (*Romans* 16.4); the Churches of Galatia (*I Corinthians* 16.1; *Galatians* 1.2); the Churches of Macedonia (*II Corinthians* 8.1). He calls those who brought the various collections for the poor Christians of Jerusalem the messengers of the Churches (*II Corinthians* 8.23); and he urges the Corinthians to show the fruit of their love before all the Churches (*II Corinthians* 8.24). He speaks of the care of all the Churches which is upon his own heart (*II Corinthians* 11.28).

We know that in the very early days the gatherings of the Christians must have been small, for it was not until the early third century that anything in the nature of Church buildings came into being. In the early days the Christians were still meeting in any house which had a room large enough to give them accommodation. So Paul uses the word *ekklēsia* for any particular part of the Church in any given place. Thus he speaks of the Church which is in the house of Aquila and Priscilla (*Romans* 16.5; *I Corinthians* 16.19); of the Church in Laodicea which is connected with the house of Nymphas (*Colossians* 4.15); of the Church which is in the house of Archippus (*Philemon* 2).

Paul uses the word *ekklēsia* as a description of the body of local Christians gathered together in any one place for worship and for instruction. That is a usage which comes very near to our use of the word congregation. He speaks of the unseemly things which happen when the Corinthian Christians come together in the Church (*I Corinthians* 11. 18). He holds that the prophet edifies the Church (*I Corinthians* 14.4, 5, 12), and criticises those who place too much stress on speaking with tongues, because in the Church he himself would rather speak five words with understanding than ten thousand words in an unknown tongue (*I Corinthians* 14.19). He speaks of the whole Church being assembled in one place (*I Corinthians* 14.23). He lays it down that women are to keep silent in the Church, and that it is a shame for them to speak (*I Corinthians* 14.34, 35). He speaks of the things which he ordains and teaches in every Church (*I Corinthians* 4.17; 7.17). In all these cases the word Church describes the worshipping people of Jesus Christ, met together in His name.

Lastly, Paul uses *ekklēsia* to describe the Church as a whole, the whole company of believers in Jesus Christ in every place and in every nation. He says of himself that, as far as zeal went, he was a persecutor of the Church (*Philippians* 3.6). He talks of the manifold wisdom of God being shown through the Church, and of glory being rendered unto God in the Church (*Ephesians* 3.10, 21). He speaks of Christ being the head of the Church (*Ephesians* 1.22). He speaks of the Church being subject unto Christ, and of Christ loving the Church (*Ephesians* 5.24, 25). He speaks of the Church as being the body of Christ (*Colossians* 1.24). Paul uses the word Church as an all-embracing word to include all those who have given their hearts and dedicated their lives to Jesus Christ.

Further, Paul frequently makes it clear that he does not regard the Church as a merely human organisation or institution. The Church and the Churches are the Church and the Churches of God. Twice he confesses that he persecuted

the Church of God (*I Corinthians* 15.9; *Galatians* 1.13).
When he is rebuking the contentious members of the
Church at Corinth, he says the Churches of God have no
such custom (*I Corinthians* 11.16). He tries to make the
Corinthians, who are guilty of unseemly conduct, realise
that their conduct is the equivalent of despising the Church
of God (*I Corinthians* 11.22). He speaks of the Churches of
God which are in Judæa (*I Thessalonians* 2.14); and says
that he boasts of the excellence of the faith and conduct of
the Thessalonians in the Churches of God (*II Thessalonians*
1.4). The Church may be composed of men, but it is none-
theless the Church of God. In the same way he speaks of
the Churches of God, which are in Judæa and which are in
Christ (*I Thessalonians* 2.14; *Galatians* 1.22). The Church
is in Christ and belongs to God.

In the two letters to the Corinthians there is a hint of a
development in the thought of Paul. These two letters are
addressed to The Church of God which is at Corinth (*I
Corinthians* 1.2; *II Corinthians* 1.1). The Christian community is no longer the Church of Corinth; it is the Church
of God which is at Corinth. Here there is the beginning of
the great conception that the Church is not a collection of
loosely integrated, or isolated, units; wherever a congregation may be, it is the Church of God in such and such a
place. There is now no such thing as a Church of Corinth,
or of Galatia, or of Rome; it is all the Church of God.

Two things may well have moved Paul's thinking in this
direction. (*a*) In Corinth he had to deal with the problem
of disunity; he had to deal with a situation in which the
local congregation had been split into fragments who
claimed to be of Paul, of Apollos, of Cephas (*I Corinthians*
1.12). It was Paul's conviction that the Church is a unity;
that it is not composed of different Churches and sects and
parties; that it is not even, in the last analysis, composed of
different congregations; that it is all, wherever it is, the
Church of God. (*b*) It may well be that Paul's growing
experience of the Roman Empire helped him in this direction. All over the world there were Roman colonies. A
Roman colony was not a colony in the English sense of the

term. It was not a settlement in an unknown and unexplored land; it was not a movement of pioneers out into the unknown. Rome had a custom which she followed all over the world. There were strategic places, which commanded road junctions, and from which whole areas could be controlled. In such places Rome was accustomed to settle little bands of citizens, usually composed of veterans of the army, who had served their time, and who had been granted citizenship. These colonies were the strategic centres which bound the empire together. Now the characteristic of these colonies was that, wherever they were, the Roman language was spoken, Roman dress was worn; the magistrates had Roman titles; Roman customs were followed; Roman law was observed and administered. These colonies were little bits of Rome planted throughout the world, and they were completely and proudly conscious that it was so. Wherever they were, to the ends of the earth, surrounded perhaps by barbarians, they were Rome. So Paul saw the Church, wherever it was, as the Church of God. The Church was a unity which embraced all nations, and remained the Church of God irrespective of its local habitation. The idea of the unity of the Church had taken root in Paul's mind, and was, as we shall see, to be greatly and wonderfully developed.

Before we leave the word *ekklēsia*, we have something further still to note. The word *ekklēsia* was not a creation of the christian Church. When the christian Church annexed it for its purposes, it was already a word with a history, and a double history. At that double background we must look, in order that we may see the associations which the word *ekklēsia* carried with it, and the memories which it would awaken in the minds of those who heard it.

First, the word had a Jewish background. In the Septuagint, the Greek version of the Hebrew Scriptures, the word *ekklēsia* is regularly used for the assembled people of Israel, that is for the assembled people of God. It is, for instance, used of the assembly of the people on the day when the ten commandments were given by God to Moses. The Book of Deuteronomy speaks of " all the words, which the Lord spake with you in the mount out of the midst of the fire in

the day of the assembly (*ekklēsia*)" (*Deuteronomy* 9.10;
18.16). Frequently the word is used for the *assembly* or the
congregation of Israel (*Deuteronomy* 31.30; *Judges* 20.2; *I
Samuel* 17.47; *I Kings* 8.14; *Psalm* 22.22). So, then, for a
Jew this word had always meant *the assembled people of
God*. The very use of this word carries with it the implication that the Church is the people of God. Israel was God's
chosen people; but Israel had failed to recognise and to
accept God's Son, when he came; Israel had therefore lost
her place and her privilege as a nation. The real Israel,
the new Israel, the true people of God, the genuine *ekklēsia*
was no longer the nation of Israel; it was the Church. The
very word *ekklēsia* lays it down that it is the christian
Church which is the true instrument and agent of God.

Second, the word had a Greek background. In the great
Greek democracies the ruling body was called the *ekklēsia*,
and the *ekklēsia* consisted of every citizen who had not lost
his rights as a citizen. It is true that in the days of the
oligarchies the *ekklēsia* might be limited to those who had
some kind of property qualification; but in the great days of
the democracy the *ekklēsia* was composed of all free men
who were citizens of their city. It was the *ekklēsia* which
elected and deposed the magistrates, which received and
sent out ambassadors, and which had the last word in the
administration of justice and the making of the laws. So to
a Greek the word *ekklēsia* would tell of the glories of citizenship; and, when the Christians took over the word, the
member of the *ekklēsia*, if he were a Greek, could think of
himself most easily and most naturally as a citizen of the
kingdom of heaven.

It is seldom that the great historical national ideals of
two lines of culture meet as they do in the word *ekklēsia*.

By this time we are able to set down one of the great basic
facts about the Church, a simple fact and an obvious fact,
yet a fact often forgotten. Nowhere in the New Testament
does the word Church mean a building. In the New Testament the Church is never a structure, composed of stones
and lime, or bricks and mortar. If the reference were to a
building, no New Testament would have understood the

phrase "a *beautiful* Church". In the New Testament the Church is always a company of worshipping people who have given their hearts and pledged their lives to Jesus Christ. Since this is so we shall find information as to the true nature and function of the Church in the words which Paul uses to describe the members of the Church. Three titles for the members of the Church constantly recur in his letters.

1. The most frequent title of all is the title *saints*. In Paul's letters the members of the Church are called *saints* almost forty times. The Greek word is *hagios,* and to modern ears *saint* is an unfortunate translation. To very many people nowadays the word *saint* brings thoughts of figures in stained-glass windows, and of people surrounded with a halo of other-worldly goodness. *Hagios* is the word which is also translated *holy*; and the basic idea in it is the idea of *difference* from ordinary things, that of being set apart from ordinary purposes. So the Temple was *holy* because it was *different* from other buildings; a priest was *holy* because he was *set apart* and, therefore, *different* from other men; an animal destined for sacrifice was *holy,* because it was *different* from other animals in that it was *set apart* for a sacred purpose; the Sabbath day was *holy* because it was *different* from other days; and God is supremely the *holy One* because he is different from men. So, then, to say that the Church member is *hagios, holy,* a saint as the Authorized Version has it, is to say that he is different from other men.

No sooner have we said that than we must immediately add another thing to it. That difference is expressed, not by withdrawing from the world, but by living differently within the world. Frequently Paul gives a local habitation to the people whom he entitles *hagios.* He writes to all that are at Rome, called to be saints (*Romans* 1.7). He speaks of the poor saints which are at Jerusalem (*Romans* 15.26). He writes to all the saints that are in all Achaia (*II Corinthians* 1.1). Whatever the difference may be, that difference is meant to be expressed in the everyday life of the place where a man finds himslf, and does not consist in a withdrawal from the world after the example of the hermits, the monks and the nuns.

Wherein, then, does this essential difference consist? More than once Paul adds to the word *hagios* a defining phrase. He writes to the saints *in Christ Jesus* who are at Philippi (*Philippians* 1.1), and in the same letter he sends the closing greeting : " Salute every saint who is *in Christ Jesus* " (*Philippians* 4.21). He writes to the saints and faithful brethren *in Christ* which are at Colosse (*Colossians* 1.2). So, then, a saint is one who is in Christ Jesus. The difference which the word *hagios* expresses is that the man who is *hagios* lives his life in the constant presence of Jesus Christ, in the constant awareness of that presence, and in the constant and deliberate attempt to listen to the commands of Christ and to carry them out. His life is lived within the world, and within the affairs of the world, but his whole life is dictated by the standards of Christ, and not by the standards of the world. The word *saints* really means " Christ's dedicated people ". Those who are members of the Church are those who have dedicated their lives to Jesus Christ.

2. Almost, if not quite, as common a title for the Christians in Paul's letters is *the brethren*. When he writes to the Christians at Rome, he greets certain people by name, then he adds : " Salute the brethren which are with them " (*Romans* 16.14). To set a bad example is to sin against the brethren (*I Corinthians* 8.12). " All the brethren greet you," he writes to the Corinthians (*I Corinthians* 16.20). He speaks of the brethren who came from Macedonia (*II Corinthians* 11.9). The Letter to the Ephesians comes to its close with the blessing : " Peace be to the brethren " (*Ephesians* 6.23). " Salute the brethren which are at Laodicea," he writes to the Colossians (*Colossians* 4.15), and to the Thessalonians he writes : " Greet all the brethren with a holy kiss " (*I Thessalonians* 5.26). Throughout all his letters Paul's commonest and favourite address to the people to whom he writes is : " Brethren !"

Herein lies the great truth that the Church is meant to be a band of brothers. It is meant to be the family of God in which men are brethren one of another. When a Church is divided in spirit and in heart, when bitterness has invaded its fellowship, when the unforgiving spirit has caused breaches which remain unhealed, the Church ceases to be a Church, for a Church is no Church unless it be a brotherhood. Nelson in his dispatches attributed one of his greatest victories to the fact that he had the happiness to command a band of brothers. The Church is meant by God to be a band of brothers.

3. Less commonly, but still quite often, the Christians are *the believers, those who believe*. God is the Father of all those who believe (*Romans* 4.11). The Thessalonians in their faith and love are an example to all who believe (*I Thessalonians* 1.7).

That is to say, the Church member is the man who accepts what Jesus Christ says as true, and who lives his life on the confident assumption that it is true. The Christian is the man who is convinced that Jesus Christ is the Saviour of his soul, and who has made Jesus Christ the Lord of his life.

So, then, in regard to the world, the Church member is the man who is different, because he lives in the presence of, and according to the standards of Christ. In regard to his fellow men, the Church member is the man who lives in the fellowship of brotherhood. In regard to Jesus Christ, the Church member is the man who has accepted the offer of Christ for his soul, and the demand of Christ for his life.

We must now turn to certain great pictures of the Church which Paul uses in his letters. From them we will learn more of Paul's conception of the Church than from any other source; but, at the same time, we must be careful to remember that they are pictures and metaphors, and that too much must not be read into them, or built upon them. As we study them, the difficulty will always be to be sure when the metaphor is a metaphor, and when it is a literal fact. We shall begin with the greatest of the pictures, the picture of the Church as a living body.

Paul uses the picture of the Church as a body to stress the essential unity of the Church. He writes to the Christians at

Rome : " As we have many members in one body, and all members have not the same office, so we, being many, are one body in Christ, and everyone members one of another " (*Romans* 12.4, 5). So every man must fully use the gift which God has given him, the gift of prophecy, the gift of service, the gift of exhortation, the gift of liberality, the gift of administration, the gift of mercy (*Romans* 12.7, 8). Now it must be clearly noted out of what situation this Pauline picture arises. He has just been insisting that no man must think of himself more highly than he ought, but that he must think of himself in terms of the gifts and the graces which God has given to him to lay at the common service of the community (*Romans* 12.3). So, then, the Church is a unity like a body. No man must be conceitedly proud of any gift which God has given to him; no man must think his gift the most important, and magnify and exalt it at the expense of the gifts of others. All gifts must be used in the spirit of humility and of service, in the constant remembrance that we are never in competition with one another, but that we are like the members of one body, all of which must work in harmony and co-operation.

Paul works out this picture even more fully and vividly in *I Corinthians* 12. The Church, like the body, is composed of many members. Each member has its function. The foot cannot do without the ear; nor the ear without the eye. The body could not function at all, if it were composed entirely of one member. Even the members which are hidden, and which it would be shameful to mention and to display, have a special and peculiar honour of their own. When one member of the body suffers, it does not suffer in lonely isolation, for its suffering affects the whole body, and is of necessity shared by the whole body (*I Corinthians* 12.12-27). Once again, it must be clearly remembered out of what situation this picture arose. The Church of Corinth was doubly divided. It was divided into sects and parties who had attached themselves to the names of different people, people who were in no way responsible for the divisions, but whose names, all against their will, had been annexed by these competing parties (*I Corinthians* 1.12).

Further, as *I Corinthians* 14 shows, within the Church there was a kind of piously unholy competition in regard to spiritual gifts. Those with the gift of tongues prided themselves on it; and even the prophets competed with each other for an opportunity to deliver their message. In *I Corinthians* 12 Paul, in fact, lists the various gifts. There is the word of wisdom and the word of knowledge; there is faith, there is the gift of healing and of performing miracles; there is prophecy, the discerning of spirits, the gifts of tongues and of the interpreting of tongues (*I Corinthians* 12.7-9). Within the functions of the members of the Church there are apostles, prophets, teachers, those with the gifts of miracles, of healings, of helps, of administration, of tongues (*I Corinthians* 12.28, 29). The trouble at Corinth was that the gifts of the Spirit were being used in competition instead of in co-operation. Even at the Lord's Supper the Church at Corinth was divided into cliques and parties and sections (*I Corinthians* 11.18); and the result was that the whole effect of the sacrament was ruined, because they came together not discerning that they were the Lord's body, not sensitively aware of their intimate unity in Christ.

The immediate purpose which Paul has in using the picture of the body in this great passage of *I Corinthians* has nothing to do with the Church at large; and it has everything to do with the life and spirit of the particular congregation. Within their own assembly the Corinthians had never learned to live as one body; they were living as disintegrated and warring fragments and atoms; they were using their gifts for self-exaltation and in competition with each other; whereas they should have been living in as intimate and harmonious a state as the members of the human body. It is needless to say that that picture has in it the germ of a conception which can be, and which was to be applied, to the whole Church of Christ; but that which first produced it was in fact the warfare of a particular Church within itself.

Further, the Church is a body in the sense that it is the begetter of unity. The great letter of the Church is the

Letter to the Ephesians. The theme of this letter may be summed up in this way. As we see it, this world is a warring disunity. There is war between nation and nation, between faith and faith, between Gentile and Jew, and within a man's own being. It is the aim of God to reconcile and to gather all men and all things into one in Jesus Christ (*Ephesians* 1.10). Jesus Christ is God's instrument in the reconciliation of all the warring and divided things and persons into a new unity. By his life and by death Jesus Christ brought to men the means towards that unity. But the means towards that unity have to be brought out throughout the world to all men; and that task is the task of the Church. In the Church there is one body (*Ephesians* 4.4); Christ is the peace of men; he has gathered together Gentile and Jew within the Church; the middle wall of partition has been broken down; and they are reconciled into one body within the Church. That is to say, to put it briefly, Jesus Christ is God's instrument of reconciliation; and the Church is Jesus Christ's agent of reconciliation. The Church is meant within itself to be one body in its unity, and it is meant to be the begetter of that unity among men.

But Paul does much more than call the Church a body; he calls it by its greatest of titles—the body of Christ. Here is the great phrase which begins in *I Corinthians,* but which runs through the later letters to the *Ephesians* and to the *Colossians.* "Now," says Paul, "ye are the body of Christ, and members in particular" (*I Corinthians* 12.27). He speaks of the Church which is Christ's body (*Ephesians* 1.23); he speaks about the edifying of the body of Christ (*Ephesians* 4.12). He speaks of Jesus Christ as the head of the body (*Colossians* 1.18); and of Christ's body which is the Church (*Colossians* 1.24).

Here we come upon one of the very real problems of Pauline interpretation. There is more than one view of what Paul meant when he spoke of the Church as the body of Christ. There are those who believe that this phrase must be taken in a mystical sense, and that when a man enters into the Church of Christ, in a mystical sense he enters into the body of Christ. In a famous phrase the Church has been described as " an extension of the Incarnation ", so that just as God was Incarnate in Jesus Christ, Jesus Christ is incarnate in the Church. On the other hand there are those who believe that this phrase is to be taken in a much more practical sense, and in what might be called a functional sense. The work of Jesus Christ must go on; but he himself is no longer here in the flesh to do it; for he has returned to his glory. If Jesus Christ wants a child taught, he must find a man or a woman to teach that child. If he wants his message brought to people who have never heard it, he must find a man or a woman to take it. If he wants his help and his comfort brought to mankind, he must find those who are willing to be channels for them. That is to say, Jesus Christ needs the Church as his body, in the sense that in the Church he must find hands to do his work, feet to run upon his errands, a voice to speak his message. The Church must be the body through which Christ acts. It is, of course, true that these two views of the meaning of the phrase the body of Christ are not mutually exclusive, but the direction in which a man lays his stress and his emphasis does make a difference.

Let us for the moment leave the answer to that question of difference of meaning in abeyance, and let us return to Paul's pictures of the Church.

In Ephesians and Colossians Paul has another frequently recurring idea—the idea of Christ as the head of the Church. God has given Christ to be the head over all things to the Church (*Ephesians* 1.22). The members of the Church must grow up into him who is the head, that is Christ (*Ephesians* 4.15). As the husband is head of the wife, so Christ is head of the Church (*Ephesians* 5.23). Christ is the head of the body, that is the Church (*Colossians* 1.18). He is the head by which all the body is nourished and administered and knit together (*Colossians* 2.19). We may note also that Jesus Christ is called the Saviour of the body (*Ephesians* 5.23).

Now one thing emerges from all this. If we take the phrase, the Body of Christ, in its mystical sense, if we

regard the Church as the extension of the Incarnation, then
it does mean that in some sense Jesus Christ is identified
with the Church. With Paul that is not so; there is always
a clear and definite distinction between Christ and the
Church. Christ is the Saviour of the body (*Ephesians* 5.23).
The Church is subject unto Christ (*Ephesians* 5.24). The
body is the instrument through which the decisions and
purposes of the head are carried out; the body is the agent
of the head. The body is that without which the head is
practically helpless. It seems to us to be almost beyond
doubt that it is in this sense that Paul calls the Church the
Body of Christ. The Church is the instrument, the agent,
the weapon, the organism through which the purposes and
the plans of Jesus Christ must be carried out. It is through
the Church that Jesus Christ seeks to bring life and light
and salvation to men. Herein is the glory of the Church,
that the Church is the necessary instrument in the hands of
Christ.

There are two passages in Paul's letters which specially
bear this out. It may be objected that to hold that the
Church is the instrument or agent through which and by
which Jesus Christ carries out the purposes and the plans of
God is nothing less than to say that Jesus Christ is dependent on the Church. Startling as it may seem, that is precisely what Paul does say. Writing to the Colossians Paul
says that he rejoices in his sufferings for them and that he
" fills up that which is behind (lacking) of the afflictions of
Christ in his flesh for his body's sake, which is the Church "
(*Colossians* 1.24). It may seem an extraordinary thing to
say that there is something lacking in the sufferings of
Christ. What Paul means is this. Christ once and for all
found the remedy for sin; but that remedy has to be brought
to men and made known to men and offered to men—and
that is the work of Paul and the work of the Church. And
if the task of bringing the good news of God's offered salvation in Christ to men involves sufferings, these sufferings
may well be said to be the completing of the sufferings of
Christ. Let us take an analogy. A scientist or a doctor
may discover a new cure for some hitherto incurable illness;

a surgeon may discover a new technique for some hitherto
impossible operation; but the cure and the technique have
not only to be *discovered*; they must also be made *available*
to those who need them; and the making of them available
may well involve labour and sacrifice and toil and thought
which are at least comparable with the price paid for the
discovery itself. The plain fact is, that what Christ did for
men cannot avail for men until men know of it; and they
cannot know of it until the Church tells them. "How then
shall they call on him in whom they have not believed? and
how shall they believe in him of whom they have not heard?
and how shall they hear without a preacher?" (*Romans*
10.14). Christ needs the Church to bring to men the
knowledge of the salvation he offers, and that which is suffered in that task fills up and completes the sufferings of
Christ. Once again we are forced to the conception of the
Church as the agent and instrument of Christ.

The second passage is in the Letter to the Ephesians.
There Paul writes, as the Authorized Version has it, of the
Church, "which is his body, the fullness of him that filleth
all in all" (*Ephesians* 1.23). Now this is no easy statement,
and scholars are not agreed as to what it means. But, as we
see it, the simplest and the most natural meaning of it, as far
as the Greek goes, is this. The word which the Authorized
Version translates *fullness* is *plērōma*. The noun *plērōma*
comes from the verb *plērown*, which means to *fill*; and a
plērōma is that which results when something is filled.
Plērōma is used, for instance, for the filling of a cup. Euri-
pides (*The Trojan Women* 823) poetically describes the
office of a cup-bearer : " Child of Laomedon, thou hast the
filling of the cups, an office fair." Again, *plērōma* is often
used for a ship's crew or a ship's complement, as it is also
used of a ship's cargo. It is used naturally and regularly
for a basketful or a handful. Still again, in his *Politics*
Aristotle describes how Socrates had outlined the organisation of a city at its simplest (*Politics* 4.4). Socrates had laid
it down that the simplest city must contain six artisans—a
weaver, a husbandman, a shoemaker, a builder, a smith, a
herdsman, to which must be added a merchant, and a retail

dealer. These, says Aristotle, compose the *plērōma* of a city. Without them a city cannot be; with them there is the essential basis of a city. So, then, the simplest, and, indeed the commonest meaning of the Greek word *plērōma* may be expressed by the English word *complement*; the *plērōma* is that by which something is filled up, or completed. So, then, what Paul is saying is that *the Church is the complement of Jesus Christ*. The Church is that through which the task of Christ is completed. We must make it clear that we are drawing a clear distinction between the work of Christ and the task of Christ. The *work* of Christ was completed once and for all upon the Cross, for there the salvation of men was once and for all secured; but the *task* of Christ remains, and the task is to make known that saving act and all its benefits to all mankind. And it is the task of Christ which the Church must complete; it is in the completing of that task that the Church is the complement of Christ.

We hold that when Paul speaks of the Church as the Body of Christ the main emphasis of his thought is on the function of the Church as the instrument and agent of Jesus Christ, the essential complement through which Christ makes known to all men that which he has already done. It is just here that the other meaning of the Body of Christ comes in. If the Church is to complete that task, if she is to be worthy of that task, if she is to do the work for which Jesus Christ designed her, then she must live so close to Christ, she must be so much in Christ, that her unity with him is such that she can be called nothing less than the Body of Christ in the mystical sense of the term. In other words, to be the Body of Christ in the practical sense the Church must be the Body of Christ in the mystical sense also.

But we have by no means come to the end of the great Pauline pictures of the Church. One of the loveliest pictures in Paul's letters is the picture of the Church as the *Bride of Christ*. That picture is most clearly painted in *Ephesians* 5.22-23, where the relationship of husband and wife is said to be the same as the relationship between Christ and the

Church. "Husbands, love your wives as Christ loved the Church" (*Ephesians* 5.25). That conception emerges, on the surface less obviously, but even more vividly when the picture is seen in *II Corinthians* 11.2. There Paul writes to the Corinthian Christians in explanation of the urgency of his appeals, "I am jealous over you with godly jealousy; for I have espoused you to one husband, that I may present you as a chaste virgin to Christ."

In a Jewish wedding there were two important persons who were called "the friends of the bridegroom". One represented the bridegroom and one the bride. They acted as intermediaries; they conveyed the invitations to the guests; they generally looked after all the arrangements. But they had one duty which was far more important than any other—it was their duty to guarantee the chastity of the bride; it was their duty to assure the bridegroom of the purity and the virginity of the bride. So Paul thinks of Christ as the bridegroom, and of himself as the friend of the bridegroom, and of the Church of Corinth as the bride who is being prepared for Christ; and Paul sees it as his task that he must present the Church at Corinth a pure and unspotted bride to Jesus Christ.

This is a conception which goes far back, and which has its roots in the Old Testament. The prophets saw Israel as the Bride of God. "Thy Maker is thy husband; the Lord of hosts is his name" (*Isaiah* 54.5). "Surely as a wife treacherously departeth from her husband, so have ye dealt treacherously with me, O house of Israel, saith the Lord" (*Jeremiah* 3.20). That is why the Old Testament so often speaks of spiritual infidelity as adultery, and that is why, when Israel is unfaithful, she is said "to go a-whoring after strange gods" (*Exodus* 34.15, 16; *Deuteronomy* 31.16; *Psalm* 73.27; *Hosea* 9.1); and it is that spiritual infidelity to God that Jesus spoke of when he spoke of "an evil and *adulterous* generation" (*Matthew* 12.39; 16.4; *Mark* 8.38). And that is why in the Old Testament God can so often be called a *jealous* God (*Deuteronomy* 32.21; *Exodus* 20.5; 34.14; *Zechariah* 8.2). God is the lover who can brook no rival.

Here we have the loveliest of all the pictures of the relationship between Christ and the Church. The Church is the Bride of Christ; the relationship between Christ and the Church is as intimate as the relationship between man and wife. Nothing less than the closest of all ties will suffice as an analogy of the relationship between Christ and his Church.

There still remain certain other titles for the Church in Paul's letters at which we must look.

Christians are *members of the family of God* (*oikeioi theou*). Paul writes to the Ephesians that they are no more strangers, but they are fellow-citizens with the saints, and members of the household of God (*Ephesians* 2.19). It is of the greatest significance to note how the relationship between the Christian and the Church and God is described in terms of the closest and most intimate human relationships, in nothing less than terms of husband and of wife, and of father and of child.

Sometimes in Paul's letters the Church is described in terms of a building, erected by and for God. " Ye are God's *building* " (*oikodome*) Paul writes to the Corinthians (*I Corinthians* 3.9). The whole Church is like a building fitly framed together (*Ephesians* 2.21).

It is from this conception that we get the idea of *edification*, which literally means *building up*. The words of the prophets build up the Church (*I Corinthians* 14.3-5). The reason why the Christians must seek to excel in spiritual gifts is not to glorify themselves, but to build up the Church (*I Corinthians* 14.12). Paul always does everything for the building up of his people, and his authority is God (*II Corinthians* 12.19; 13.10; 10.8). The christian duty is to build up one another (*I Thessalonians* 5.11), and ever to pursue the things which make for mutual upbuilding (*Romans* 14.19; 15.2). All offices and gifts are given for no other purpose than the building up of the Church (*Ephesians* 4.12, 16); and the life and conduct of the Christian must be such that it is good for building up the Church (*Ephesians* 4.29).

Here we are faced with two great truths. The work of

the Church must be always construction, and never destruction. If destruction has to take place, and if old and ingrained ideas and conceptions must be swept away, it must always be to raise something new and better in their place. All christian teaching and action must be characteristically positive and never merely negative in its aim and object. Again, it means that the Christian must never think of himself as an individual. He is a stone in a building. He is not there to draw attention to himself, but to add strength to the building of which he is a part. He is joined to his fellow-Christians as closely as stone is joined to stone in a well-compacted building.

It is further to be noted that there are passages where this building is more closely defined. The Church is not simply a building; it is a building which is *the temple of God*. "Know ye not," demands Paul, "that ye are the temple of God?" (*I Corinthians* 3.16, 17). "What agreement has the temple of God with idols?" (*II Corinthians* 6.16). The whole building is fitly framed together, and is growing into "a holy temple of the Lord" (*Ephesians* 2.21).

The idea here is very simple, and yet very great. A temple is the dwelling-place upon earth of a god; and the Church is nothing other than the earthly dwelling-place of the Spirit of God.

There are two further building metaphors in Paul's letters. First, Christ is the foundation of the Church (*I Corinthians* 3.11); and, second, Christ is the chief cornerstone of the Church (*Ephesians* 2.20). It is on Christ that the whole Church is built, and it is by Christ that the whole structure of the Church is held together.

Finally, there is one picture of the Church in Paul's letters from a quite different source. He writes to the Corinthians as the Authorized Version has it: "Ye are God's husbandry" (*I Corinthians* 3.9). The word is *gēorgion*, and it means *a field*. The Church is the soil which can become fertile in all good things, by the action of the Spirit of God upon it.

So, when we look back across Paul's thinking about the

Church, we see that for him the Church is the company of men and women who have dedicated their lives to Christ, whose relationship to Christ is as close as that of husband and of wife, whose relationship to each other is as firm as the stones within a building, and whose supreme glory is that they are the Body in whom Christ dwells, and through which he acts upon the world.